insidepoetry
Poetry from people in prison

VOLUME 1

Edited by Rachel Billington
Foreword by Andrew Motion

First published in 2009 by Inside Time Ltd

P.O. Box 251, Hedge End,
Hampshire SO30 4XJ.
Telephone: 0844 335 6483
www.insidetime.org

Inside Time is a 'not for profit' organisation

© Inside Time Ltd. All rights reserved. No part of this publication may be reproduced, stored in a retrieval system, or transmitted in any form or by any means, electronic, mechanical, photocopying, recording or otherwise without the prior permission of the copyright holders.

ISBN 978-0-9562855-0-8

Layout by Tonic Design - info@tonicdesign.net

Printed in Great Britain by the MPG Books Group, Bodmin and King's Lynn

PREFACE

These collected poems have been chosen from over 2000 sent to Inside Time over the last eighteen months.

Inside Time is the National Newspaper for Prisoners launched in 1990. It is a 'not for profit' publication that is distributed via prison libraries throughout the UK prison estate and sent to a number of British prisoners held in prisons overseas.

As the newspaper is primarily written by prisoners for prisoners, the content voices the true concerns and reflects prisoners' genuine interests - poetry being very important for many. The first published poem in Inside Time was 'Old Lags' by Noel 'Razor' Smith in 1994, which is reproduced in this collection. A regular poetry section was introduced in 2007 and immediately proved very popular. This was followed by quarterly eight page poetry supplements so more could be published.

Most of the poems in this book have been printed already, some have not. They are written by prisoners serving time in British gaols and by a few outside the U.K. They reflect our readership which is very wide: men and women, young offenders, British citizens and foreign nationals, the highly educated and those who have never read let alone written a poem before. Their subjects are as diverse as their characters and their backgrounds but they all have their present situation in common. Incarceration lies heavily on them but there is also humour and hopefulness. The letters that accompany them often thank a girlfriend, a mother or a special friend and sometimes ask for help with spelling or punctuation. They are always grateful for the opportunity to air their thoughts.

This is Inside Poetry Volume 1. We trust there will be further volumes. Each prison library has been given one copy free and copies are also available from www.insidetime.org or by writing to: Inside Time P.O.Box 251 Hedge End Hampshire SO30 4XJ.

We would like to thank everybody who has helped with this project and in particular, our first reader, Chloe Francis.

Rachel Billington
Inside Time April 2009

FOREWORD

Although education gives us a comparatively complicated language to speak about poetry, and although some poetry is itself complicated in terms of compression, allusion and technique, the thing itself is fundamentally a very primitive force. It proves the basic human need for, and delight in, like sounds - in rhythm, in metaphorical language, in the opportunity to make sense while embracing mystery, and occasionally even nonsense. We recite our first poems (without necessarily calling them poems) when we stand in the corner of the playground, chanting. The sound of that heartbeat remains in all the poetry we read through our later lives.

And in the poems we might write in later life. For some of us, that writing will be the manifestation of 'who we are': poets first and foremost. For a larger majority, poetry will be a form they turn to occasionally, or for distinct periods of their existence. This will happen because poetry, of all the literary forms, is the one best equipped to convey strong feeling – and in being so, it is also the form best able to help us enjoy and endure our time on earth.

The poems in this collection give eloquent proof of this. The circumstances of their composition have an important thing in common, and their involvement with powerful emotion is also a shared strength. And yet these base-line similarities comprise the ground in which a marvellous variety has grown. Readers will find funny poems, sad poems, introspective poems, world-wise poems – poems, in fact, which fit and realise every mood under the sun and moon. For all these reasons, the anthology is a deeply enjoyable one. Its exceptional value lies in the fact that it releases and validates the voices it contains.

Andrew Motion
Poet Laureate 1999-2009

" These poems are sad and honest and true, and they will strike a chord with all kinds of people whose captivity may be mental rather than physical. Well done Inside Time, and let's hope this volume inspires such a spirit of creative competition in our prisons that someone somewhere produces the next Ballad of Reading Gaol. "

Boris Johnson *(Mayor of London)*

" I hear so much when I read these poems. Clearly those who wrote them have much to say and the poems have unlocked thoughts and feelings which might otherwise have remained hidden and suppressed. This is poetry at its most effective, enabling people to find a voice, to say what they might not have dared to say so openly before.

Though their authors might remain locked up, at least for a while, their feelings have been freed. They have a life of their own now and their message can reach anyone with eyes to read and ears to hear. "

Michael Palin *(Author, traveller and humorist)*

" Since its launch in 1990, Inside Time has been a real voice for prisoners and also something of a showcase for their writing talent. Like so many other budding but incarcerated writers I am grateful that I was able to hone my skills on their pages. This book is a great way of showing the outside world that there is more to prisoners than what they usually read in the tabloids. Thought provoking, sad, tender, and sometimes very funny - a must read for anyone with a soul. "

Noel 'Razor' Smith *(Author and prisoner)*

CONTENTS

The Hopes of a Child and the Forbidden Dream	Adel Abdel Bary	11
Too many cooks	John Allen	12
Within The Concrete Box	Steve Arstall	13
Prison!	Shane Arthur	14
Prison	Gavin Backhouse	15
The Alarm Bell!!	A Bailey	16
Prison Facts and Fairytales	David Barlow	17
Manic Depression	Scott Barrett	18
Me	Patrick Bell	19
Day in Day Out	Wolfie Bishop	20
Freebird	Wolfie Bishop	21
Drugs don't work	Keiran Botterill	22
Metamorphosis	Dave Boyes	23
The Long Winter Nights	Dave Boyes	24
Reflections	Jimmy Brand	25
Up The Creek	Charles Briggs	26
I once met the Lord	Dean Alan Brindley	27
Smack City – Home of the grave	Gavin Broadbent	28
Autumn	J Brown	29
The clock it keeps on ticking	Adam Brumhead	30
A Nonsense Poem	Bryan (HMP YOI Moorland)	31
Windows and Bars	Adel Burns	32
Being me	Wendy Bury	33
Role Models	Shane Canning	34
I sleep in somebody's toilet	Ray Carrington	35
Punishment, Deterrent or just plain boring	Paul Cartwright	36
I'm innocent I tell you	Rachel Charlton	37,38
Living a lie	Daniel Compton	39
Happy 1st Birthday	Bernadette Coote	40
What's it all for?	Anthony Corson	41
A Mother's Heartbreak	Denise Coulman	42,43
Da Concrete man	Simon Crewe	44
HMP Lincoln	Simon Crewe	45
Loveless Weekend	Paul Crewe	46
The Special Brew Crew	Harry Cross	47
A Decision	Prudence Crouch	48
Red Head	Mr Curtis	49
Same old shit … just another day	Martyn Dance & Marc Harris	50
Prison Officer	Lisa Marie Davies	51
First Kiss	Richard Davison	52
Shell Shocked	Adam Dellicott	53
Incarceration: The Nature of the Beast	Ian Dickens	54
Nothing is ever lost	Shane Dobson	55

The Voice .... Jason Dobson	56
Nike Air Max and Flip Flops .... Randy Donegan	57
Repentance .... Shama Dookhooah	58
Fish A Wish .... Iain Doyle	59
What's special about Special Brew? .... Will Draven	60
In the dock .... HMP Usk DSMS	61
Memories .... Jaheer Duel	62
A changed man .... Jamie Dunning	63
Institutionalization .... Paul Eaton	64
I wonder .... Tony Edwards	65
Legacy .... Tony Edwards	66
Marbles .... Tony Edwards	67
Taking The Piss .... Tony Edwards	68,69
Institutionalised .... Osaleni Eubuomwan	70,71
Round and round we go!! .... Tony Evans	72
When Heroin Brings You To Your Knees .... James Farricker	73
My life .... Alma Fekete	74
Rip Offs .... Steven Fethon	75
Dé ja vu .... Jonny Fowler	76,77
I Miss Momma .... Brian Franklin Thames	78
Billie Basic! .... Tracie Frost	79
Freedom .... Mathew Gallagher	80
Mum .... M Gibbons	81
The Greedy Bankers .... Daniel Goldsmith	82
Rewind .... Robert Gray	83
The Harvest .... Robert Gray	84
Waiting .... Robert Gray	85
The way it was .... Nathan Greef	86
Try me sometime .... Steen Grundy	87
Life sentence .... Keith Hall	88
Sunday Best .... Keith Hall	89
Shhhhh .... Stuart Hall	90
If only .... Dean Hamilton	91
Living In This Grave .... Dean Hamilton	92
Drinking then jail .... Dan Hannam	93
When will I be free? .... Luke Harrison	94
My Lying Heart .... Mark Hawkins	95
Rose Tinted Spectacles .... Mark Hawkins	96
Together .... Darren Hawkins	97,98
Primal scream .... Warren Heath	99
Heroin .... Liam Hickson	100
Brave Mask .... S Hodgson	101
Who are these people? .... D Hogg	102
Hot stuff .... David Holland	103
Goodbye Girls .... Scott Hornby	104
Crack Head .... Mark Horrocks	105
Realism .... Dennis Hudson	106

Title	Author	Page
Obama Elect	Marcus Humphrey	107
Found	Paul Hutchinson	108
Burn	C Ingle	109
Second Chance	N Jarrett	110
The Sleeper	George Jenkinson	111
Despair	Tony Jennings	112
Bad day	Andy Jewitt	113
Heart of the country	M Jolley	114
Detox	Matthew Jones	115
No View	Gregory Jones	116
The Visit	Tony Joyce	117
Ruegan	Declan Kavanagh	118
Cleaner's Lament	Daniel Kessler	119
I only want to talk	Stephen Kidd	120
The Easy Life	Andrew King	121
Prison Bullshit Blues	Philip Kirk	122
Back in the day	Steve Lewtas	123
Wind scream	Paul Lumsden	124
Bumblebee	Del MacDonald	125
Speak to a Listener	Joseph MacLeod	126
Safe to cry	Gordon Maddocks	127
Interim	Carl Mallinson	128
Who's that girl?	Lorraine Manzi	129
Political Chameleon	Edward Marriette	130
Ode to a dead towel!	Stephen Marron	131
Memoirs of an illegal immigrant	Johnson Mashoko	132
Reach For The Sky	Angie Mason	133
Understanding my cell mate	Steve McCarthy	134
In Memoriam – 9/11	Gerard McGrath	135
The Test	J McHale	136
Behind these Bronzefield Walls	Naledi Moet-Lottering	137,138
A vision of hell	Kieran Mooney	139
Paranoid Prisoner	David Morris	140
One Day	Mr C (HMP Wealstun)	141
Smile	Stephen Murphy	142
The Parole Hearing	Alexander Murtly	143,144
Tottenham	Ricky Mutton	145
Me…You	Charlie Nokes	146
Love and Sorrow	Marcus O'Neill	147
Oh greedy cockroach!	Oz (HMP Maidstone)	148
Gay and proud	Paul Palmer	149
The Thief	Tony Palmer	150
Life's Deal	Ian Parkinson	151
Jack The Lad	Liam Phipps	152
Dreamer	Kevin Poole	153
Jean Sprackland came today!	Tony Pope	154
Shadow on my bars	David Prior	155

The Poem's Trap .... Abz Rauf	156
The Police Visit .... Clovis Razak	157
Mr Naughty .... Annabelle Rogers & Jackie Sheppard	158
The Light In The Tunnel .... Simon Rowe	159
Why Am I Here? .... Simon Rowe	160
It's just another day .... Mike Ruane	161
A mother's tale .... Claudia Santos	162
HMP .... Paul Sarvent	163
Lifer's life .... Andy Senior	164,165
That Thing .... Andy Senior	166
Prison ... Rehabilitation? .... Shane (HMP Downview)	167
Frail and False! .... T Shepherd	168
A Painful Visit .... Robert Shreeve	169
The Lost Years .... Robert Shreeve	170
What she says (and what she does) .... Robert Shreeve	171
Hardman .... Jason Smith	172
In my cell .... Jason Smith	173
Voyage .... Jason Smith	174
I'm So Glad I Found You .... Katie Smith	175
Ignorant Bliss .... Gerald Smith	176
Lonely Noel .... Gerald Smith	177
The Pigeon .... Gerald Smith	178
The Visit .... Gerald Smith	179
To Answer the Question .... Gerald Smith	180
Old Lags .... Noel 'Razor' Smith	181
The Hanging Basket Seeds of Hope
.... Sol, Wayne, Mark, Jahbi, Sed (HMP Grendon)	182
A dark place .... Ross Spencer	183
Skag Rat .... Tony Standen	184
Why? .... Anne Stanmore	185
You .... Paul Stellato	186
Heartache .... Stephen (HMP Ashwell)	187
Cold Steel .... Sticks (HMP Birmingham)	188
Dreams .... Syd (HMP Wellingborough)	189
Only you .... Peter Szczepanski	190
Life Through My Eyes .... Ste Tallby	191
Inmates come and go .... Neil Tangotra	192
Love has a price! .... Neil Tangotra	193
A Druggie's Life .... Neil Taylor	194,195
Old Soldiers Never Cry .... Mike Taylor	196,197
Stop The Clock .... Graeme Taylor	198
Different kinds of everyone .... Liam Thomas	199
A Seasonal Sense of Freedom .... Jason Thompson	200
Please answer me .... Danyella Thompson	201
Hewell Holiday Complex .... Adrian Tinson	202
One More Time .... Felipe Tripicchio	203
Window Warrior .... Andy Tuffs	204

Application Procedure .... Steve Twigg	205
Bang Up Blues .... P Vernon	206
Sycamore tree .... Corrinne Vincent	207
Abandonment .... Matthew Walsh	208
Cell with a view .... Matthew Walsh	209
Over .... George Watts	210
Doing time .... Haige White	211
Television Hell .... Luke Whiteman	212
Through new eyes! .... Gary Wilkinson	213
Sick Building Syndrome .... Matthew Williams	214
Evening calling .... Kevin Willis	215
Sorry .... Clayton Wilson	216
What's Missing? .... Geoff Wilson	217,218
From young, impatient blokes .... Geoff Wilson	219
Rat Race .... Ben Woodfield	220
TWOC .... Sean Woolley	221
Prison Boy .... David Wright	222
Our Hero - Olympics .... Michael Wyatt	223
Cockroach in my pad .... Anthony Young	224

The Hopes of a Child and the Forbidden Dream

My little girl, born two months after my arrest, asks,
'When can I be with you for a whole day?'
'When will you come with me to school?'
I say, 'God willing ... soon'.

That night I decide to see her in my dreams but ...
I retract ...
When I hear the guard call, 'Applications!'
I realise I must hand in my form to the governor
So that he will let me spend time
With my little girl,
In my dreams

So I look the guard in the eyes and say,
As they have taught us,
'Please excuse me. I won't go back to those dreams.'

Adel Abdel Bary - HMP Long Lartin

Too many cooks

There once was a time – the point of this rhyme
When cooking was mastered with ease
You want to cook haddock? Consult Fanny Craddock
She'll take care of the teas.

But in this day and age, TV chefs are the rage
All you need is right there on the screen
The 'F' word as well as a kitchen from hell
There's always a lot to be seen.

There's Novelli and Rhodes, Worrell-Thompson
    knows loads
And don't forget Hugh Whittingstall
Rick Stein is fine for a dinner with wine
But only James Martin won't pall.

John Burton-Race, a familiar face
When planning a dinner for eight
Take care with the cream if you don't want to dream
Of diets and ways to lose weight.

Nigella's paella, a guaranteed seller
What's more she has fabulous looks
She does things with a spoon that make grown men
    swoon
This queen of the small screen cooks.

Over in Norwich, Delia's porridge
Gives City an excellent start
While closer to home Jamie Oliver's tome
Has school dinners close to his heart.

Marco Pierre, there's a name to strike fear
In all but the stoutest of hearts
If the kitchen is hell it's best not to dwell
Just get on with the quiches and tarts.

Heston Blumenthal holds us all in thrall
With his ice cream of bacon and egg
While Ainsley's two teams are so full of beans
They have catering tops off the peg.

But Ramsay's the man whose skill with a pan
Produces a powerful broth
The problem my friend is that by the end
He'll be telling us all to F*** Off!

John Allen - HMP Gartree

Within The Concrete Box

I am not sure what's the reason
It is very hard to explain
Locked within a concrete box
Makes you feel insane

When the door is open
Your mind is free and clear
Once locked within the concrete box
You're alone with all the fear

Just one small problem
One wrong word said
Back within the concrete box
Fills your night with dread

Should you call a carer
Or should you try to be strong
The concrete box mocks you
The night can feel so long

The morning finally gets here
You rush down to the phone
The concrete box beaten
A few words and you're not alone

At last another day closer
To the day you end the strife
The concrete box behind you
It's time for real life.

Steve Arstall - HMP Altcourse

Prison!

Ask me no question I'll tell you no lie
My cell mate don't smoke and neither do I
Don't ask me for Rizla, don't ask me for burn
Go to class, get a job use the money you earn
Don't mean to sound selfish, don't mean to sound rude
I'm just tired of bang up and this shit they call food.
Potato by the plateful, potato by the bunch
They serve it here for breakfast, for dinner and for lunch.
If I see another potato it'll bring tears to my eyes
Go outside for exercise come back smelling like fries.
Give me dinner at five then lock me away
Banged up til morning with no time to play.
No chance to take a shower, now my skin feels like ash
Can't get nothing from canteen coz I ain't got no cash.
Sharing a room with druggies, killers and crazies
But at night hear them sniffling and crying like babies.
Each morning I wake up and head off to class
At night locked in a room smelling like old feet and ass
Can't see my family, my friends or my son,
Laying in my bed at night thinking what have I done.
I try to hide my pain so I just keep on smiling,
What I wouldn't give to be back on my Bahamian island
do the crime pay the time, that's what they say,
Can't hold me forever, have to send me home one day.

*Shane Arthur - **HMP The Verne***
Written when a resident of Wormwood Scrubs

Prison

Whilst sat here reading your Inside Time
Stories of laughter and people's crime

Drug reports and how they manage
Whilst now knowing they've created the damage

Prison overcrowding comes into the frame
Who's caused the problem?
Probation is to blame

Every week I hear of some new scheme
With all new rules
And all created by a board of fools

So what's becoming of this penal place
Run by morons from outer space

No more room and no more cells
They've brought this on all by themselves

For years on end I've seen such flaws
People in prison for so called laws
Laws which differ from drugs and drink
The system's struggling don't you think?

No wonder HMP can't cope
Whilst getting recalled for smoking dope!

Gavin Backhouse - HMP Frankland

The Alarm Bell!!

Everything stops when an alarm bell sounds,
Screws of all sizes run through the grounds,
All puffed up, trying to look mean and hard,
We see them coming through the yard.
Male and female, all of them sweaty, red faces,
Bulging eyes and the odd ugly Betty
They arrive on the wing jangling their keys,
Most of them knackered, weak at the knees.
Shouting their orders, which nobody hears
Because the cons respond, with sarcastic cheers.
Nobody gets caught for pressing the bell,
But it's relieved the boredom in our little hell,
Sorry officer, for spoiling your shift
But to catch the culprit you must be swift.
There is a moral to this story and the moral is
You have to run like 'Billy Whizz'

A Bailey - HMP Maidstone

Prison Facts and Fairytales

Inmates up and down the land
Tell tall tales big and grand,
Some are fact and others not
Which are which? Well who knows that?
Here's a few I've heard for you
So you decide what's lies or true.
To be a cleaner on the wing
To the screws you'll have to sing
Tell them who does this and that
And make them cups of tea to bat.
For borrowed goods the price to pay
It's 'double bubble' all the way
For half an ounce of your favourite burn
An ounce they will expect in return.
Write your name upon the wall
And you'll return to read it all
'I woz ere' is what you'll say
And ere you are another day.
Jailhouse lawyers know the best
But their advice won't pass the test
They'll send you off to court with hope
Only to return a sentenced dope.
The screws can't stop the clock from ticking
Despite all of their grief and bickering
Closed visits, basic, down the block
None of these will stop the clock.
So when you're caught committing crime
End up in the dock, down the line
Remember if you're refused bail
These prison facts and fairytales.

David Barlow - HMP Leeds

Manic Depression

There is too much
A thousand grim winters
Grow in my head
In my ears
The sound of the coming dead
All seasons, all same
All living, all pain
No opiate to lock still
My senses
Only left, the body locked tenser

Scott Barrett - HMP Wayland

Me

Sometimes I am angry
Sometimes I am mad
Sometimes I am quiet
Sometimes I am sad

When I get angry
I punch, kick and swear
I hurt lots of people
And I don't really care

When I get mad
I throw things on the floor
I shout out stupid things
And slam my bedroom door

When I am quiet
I'm thinking what I've done
If I didn't do these things
I would have much more fun

When I am sad
I want to make things right
I'd really like a cuddle
I don't want to fight

I want to change
I'll do my best
I want to be just
Like the rest.

Patrick Bell - HMP Stafford

Day in Day Out

Day in, tick tock, seconds drip away, just like my
leaky tap. No rhythm.
Paint by numbers, talk in riddles, life in tatters.
This is jail, be grateful for the food
Don't compliment the chef,
No tip for the waiter, this is jail
Where silver fish slither then vanish silently
Into piss-stained lino cracks.
Drop the soap? Give up hope, buy another bar.
Chains on your mind, shackles on your tongue, razor wire,
Locks and bars, twist and shout. Let me out.
Shaved heads, metal beds, this is jail.
Brewed fruits, smoked herbs. Healing powers. Out of hours.
Dreams of girls, forgotten passion. The call of home is loud
Still as loud, not allowed.
Surrounded by; cheating, lying, two-faced bullies but
To them it's just a job, this is jail.
They bend the rules, make another one. No black,
No white, grey matter. Doesn't matter, this is jail.
No voice. No face, no reflection, no mirror
No trust, no fun, no end in sight. Memories.
Surname, number. Identity loss, greedy boss,
Exploitation, third world wages, cutbacks, knockbacks
Pair of Jacks. Poker. Joker. Smoker.
Fantasist, journalist, another fairy tale
There is life on Mars, this is jail.
Scant regard, disregard, watch your back, this is jail.
Out of bounds, haunting sounds. Dead of night
Drum and bass, loss of face
Saving grace, what's gone is gone,
Absent friends sit beneath the same moon I watch at night.
Waiting, tick tock, unlock, broken clock. Day out.

Wolfie Bishop - HMP Littlehey

Freebird

They're here throughout the year, eating scraps of bread.
Well, just the other morning, while I was still in bed
An incident took place that wasn't in my dreams
It's true I tell you, no matter how it seems.
Not a common sight, I'm sure as sure can be
For the first time that day I saw a duck, sitting in a tree.
At first I only heard him, in fact the bastard woke me up.
Lookin' round for missiles I grabbed an apple, then a cup.
I scanned below my window whilst standing on my bed,
To get the perfect shot and bounce them off his head.
But this rowdy little quacker was hidden far too well,
And from where the noise was coming, I really couldn't tell.
The squawking was relentless, more prisoners grew irate,
The love for ducks we had, quickly turned to hate.
Morning unlock came around and we all began the search,
'til at last the beast was spotted on it's lofty perch.
Big Stuart was the first on scene, shouting out aloud,
'Look up there' he cried, 'it's in a tree, sitting peacock proud'.
'Yeah right', I said, then looked once and did a double take.
There it was, this bloody duck who'd kept us all awake.
T'was far enough away, our fruit just wouldn't reach.
So Mr Mallard carried on, with his noisy, ducky speech.
The foliage was far too thick, I wondered where he'd put his feet,
Must've stopped right where he landed, using branches as a seat.
Then I thought about this duck, sitting in a tree,
Maybe he's got stuck up there, imprisoned just like me.
Perhaps the quacks were cries for help from this stranded drake,
I just wanna go back home, he's longing for his lake.
Now ducks can fly well enough, once they get a-going,
But usually need more take off room than a double decker Boeing.
So how he's getting down again, I really couldn't say.
I didn't see it happen, but he must've found a way.
We'd moved away by then, driven crazy by the sound,
When suddenly all went quiet, the feeling quite profound.
I ran along the landing to take another look
And standing there was just the tree, without the bloody duck!

Wolfie Bishop - HMP Littlehey

I've gotta share this story, which I swear is based on fact
'bout a duck at Littlehey, with which the grounds are packed.

Drugs don't work

The sun's going under
Should we really wonder
If we're heading for danger
When we meet a stranger
Somehow we're walking
Someone's done the talking
We continue the chancing
Hearts stop for dancing
Moons up high now
We survive somehow
Taking the bad moves
Just for the good moods
Whispering voices
Startled by choices
Out begging for coppers
Ones that won't stop us
Skanking for profit
Wanna come off it
Is it desire
Drugs take you higher
Ya getting much slower
Have they taken over
They've beaten ya head now
Not long till ya dead now
Six feet under
No-one will wonder
Can you blame them
When you betrayed them
No funeral starting
No crowds are parting
Ya soon been forgotten
Ya decayed and ya rotten
So ya dead now
Hear what I said now
I said ya dead now
Cold earths ya bed now
Heaven don't want ya
Hell don't need ya
There's no more joking
On dry mud ya choking
This is the ending
No more is pending
Gotta end somehow
And it ends now.

Keiran Botterill -
HMP/YOI Norwich

Metamorphosis

A frightful time when in the mirror you see
The excuse of a person you wanted to be.
A realisation that you need to evolve
Before you become like the last man, and he dissolved.
Stand out from the crowd and prove everyone wrong
You're not the same person that you've been for so long.
A moment of clarity, or an act of fate?
Either way, remember, it's never too late!
Don't be so eager to prove to the Earth
That a life behind bars is all you are worth.
Instead, be inspired by the spirit within
And prove to the world that you too can win.
It's always so easy to choose the life that you know
But life is so boring when you go with the flow.
Instead, be an example for the generation to come
And show a life of crime is really just dumb.
Criminals exist, but real people live
Criminals take, but real people give.
A man is defined by the choices he makes
And learning from life ... all his mistakes.
Don't have regrets, put them to use
There are too many people that use their past as an excuse.
Aim for the stars, from the depths of the sea
And then be the person that you aspire to be.
What I'm trying to say is that your life is not set
There's a new you inside; one that I have just met.

Dave Boyes - HMP Wellingborough

The Long Winter Nights

The long winter nights, everlasting and cold,
When you need someone special to love and to hold,
When the snow starts to fall and the trees look so bare,
The house fills with love and with presents to share.
When Christmas time comes, and a time to reflect,
On the year that has passed and the one to expect.
Those long winter nights with the days gone too soon,
And the world is lit up by the shine of the moon.
When animals hide until the dawn of spring,
And when all children wonder, what Santa will bring.
When the chimes of Big Ben welcome a New Year,
And it dawns on people the last one was a blur.
When people share love, on the 14th of month two,
And when it's most common to say, 'I do'.
When the coming of the spring in March is nigh,
You kiss those long winter nights a sincere goodbye.

Dave Boyes - HMP Wellingborough

Reflections

They gave me a mirror, hangs on my cell wall,
The person stood before me someone I cannot recall,
Clear eyes, pearl teeth, like a film star, not a cellmate I'd pick or choose,
He reminds me of someone I once knew before getting high on the booze.
Every time I go for a drink, he's there, watching, above my sink,
He mimics me when I shave, why don't he just behave?
The more I stare into his face, the more he seems right on my case,
Smirking back his insidious smile, giving it cunning and treacherous guile.
He's boxing clever, there's nowhere to hide,
Do I make out he's not there and swallow my pride?
Is he me serving it large, artful, cunning, always in charge.
Full of himself, surfing the high, no fake, cheap copy living a lie.
Mirrored image, bold and clear, no longer the lesser, hooked on gear.
Which of us stays, who? Banished to go,
Withering fast, watching him grow,
Lost to perish upon his curse, who will prevail to finish the verse?
Do I fare from whence I came? Bathed in Hades' flame,
Fading away, headed to hell … reflecting from a solitary cell.

Jimmy Brand - HMP Highdown

Up The Creek

We've come from the Limpopo
And the Congo and the Tees
And the Mersey and the Ebro
And streams on the Pyrenees
We have canoed down the Amazon
And punted on the Isis
And we've borne the Severn's troubles
And the Volga's mid-life crisis
We've paddled in the Indus
And we've dined beside the Rhine
We've cavorted by the Danube
And we've seen the Shannon shine
Now we're becalmed of our own choice
And our horse has lost its saddle
Our lifeboat has run aground
We're up the creek without a paddle.

Charles Briggs - HMP The Verne

HMP The Verne has a large proportion of foreign nationals, hence the inspiration for this poem.

I once met the Lord

I once met the Lord at HMP Bristol
I wasn't on drugs, my thoughts were quite crystal
He stopped me one day for an ear to lend
He lived on the threes, two cells from the end.
I asked him how long was he serving inside?
To the end of existence and time he replied.
He switched on his kettle as I pulled up a pew,
Coffee? He said, with a biscuit or two?
I sat there puzzled why the Lord was in jail?
As I noticed the scars on his hands from the nails.
His clothes were old and torn and tattered,
His hair and beard were long and matted.
His face was gaunt, and his eyes were kind,
But the same question kept echoing round my mind.
So Lord I said please put me at rest,
Tell me why they've locked up the best?
The answer to that is easy my son,
It's for fighting a battle that's not yet won.
I'm also charged with supplying he said
As he began to unscrew the leg from his bed,
Supplying what? I asked confused,
As he lit up a spliff and looked amused.
He screwed the leg back on his bed,
Then placed his hands upon my head.
Supplying forgiveness and hope to all man,
And I'm dealing just as much as I can.
I was honoured the Lord chose to talk with me,
So I left his cell with pride and with glee,
But I stopped and looked back once more with a sigh,
For the card on his door had caught my eye,
It read as follows: Lord 748,
So had I spoke with the Lord or another inmate?

Dean Alan Brindley - HMP Garth

Smack City - Home of the Grave

It's called smack city, the place where I live
Where every soul's lost and no-one can forgive
Where poverty's not history, with cameras on every street
And police ignore crimes and never walk a beat
Heroin is normal 'n police raids are daily
Smack city's a place just set up to fail me
Locks on every window, barricades on the door
Piss on the stairways 'n needles on every floor
Domestics in every house, kids told that they'll be nothing
Brutality and violence, coz freedom is in the coffin
Young mothers roam the city, lookin for a hit
Destined for death, never leaving this pit
This city's broken, no council can mend
Everyone knows everyone but no-one's gotta friend
Coz heroin is their only true friend in life
It's a dog eat dog city so everyone's got a knife
No good from Gordon, not even when it was Blair
A forgotten city, where no-one's gotta care
Street crime to murder, ram raids 'n theft
Smack city's a place with no honesty left
From Leo to Pisces, Scorpios and Aries
Escape is drugs, getting high with the fairies
Heroin or crack, everyone's got an addiction
When there's a draught, the whole city's in friction
The home of the hopeless! The land of the brave
Premature deaths, the home of the grave
An army of dealers for the army of users
Dealers live large, while H kills the abusers
Drug squads can't stop it, no matter what they've got
Even if they stop the brown, they'll never stop the rock
Prostitution's on the rise, the girls are getting younger
This lost city will put me six feet under
It rains everyday, a place where no-one smiles
Addict mothers leave their kids to paedophiles
Smack head dads rob their own of their goods
The grass is not green 'n flowers are just buds
No 'leccy' tonight, another candle lit dinner
All classed as losers, never seen as winners
No-one's got a job so they use drugs 'n crime
Claiming on benefits, until the end of time
No qualifications an they probably will never be
So please God Almighty set smack city free!!!!
Rest in peace to everyone who's lost through drugs
And all who've died at the hands of the curse: Heroin!

Gavin Broadbent - HMYOI Hindley

Autumn

A prisoner of conscience I ache with guilt
In a prison called autumn I'm destined to wilt
A flower on the hillside a dance in the breeze
Devoid of my freedom I'm down on my knees.

And the flower won't blossom nor beauty will bloom
Your eyes have forgotten my world is a room
And for years and for years I have toiled with a strife
And I took it for granted that this is my life.

Like autumn a soul mate of summer and spring
I dream of a heaven that love swore to bring
Now I think of the seasons
The flower on the hill
With its hands full of reasons time
Probably will

J Brown - HMP Manchester

The clock it keeps on ticking

I miss so many things
About the world outside
Now I rot here in this ten foot box
Stripped of dignity and pride

Here I'm just a number
Not a person anymore
An object in the system
Life is a daily chore

They can slam the door behind me
And leave me in the grime
They can take away my privileges
But they cannot stop the time

Someday I'll be walking free
Breathing clean air once again
The clock it keeps on ticking
So I'll just exist 'til then.

Adam Brumhead - HMP Moorland

A Nonsense Poem

I come from a place far away
Where day is night and night is day
The horses moo and eagles bark
Dark is light and light is dark
The summer isn't hot but very cold
Very old men are ten years old
The grass is blue the sky is green
It's the strangest place I've never been
Near is far and far is near
Where over there is over here
Months last only one week long
The strong are weak but the weak are strong
Small is big and big is small
Our smallest people are really tall
Yes I come from a place far away
Where day is night and night is day

Bryan - HMP YOI Moorland

Windows and Bars

At night I watch through my windows and bars
I can't see any passing cars
There aren't any people walking on the path
I can't hear any person laugh
Just looking up at an isolated place
With a sad smile plastered on my face
No stars to look at in the night sky
Listening only to the wind blow by
Watching the leaves falling from the trees
Feeling the coolness of the breeze

Adel Burns - HMP Newhall

Being me

I like to live alone
I like to
Soak in the bath
For two hours,
A trashy novel
A glass of wine
In my hand.

I like to
Stay up late
Not doing much,
Lie on the sofa
ACD on
Listening to my favourite band.

I like to
Be free
To be me,
Watch what I want
On TV
See who I want to see.

I like to live alone
Just me.

Wendy Bury -
HMP Low Newton

Role Models

Hi, I'm a pop star, everything is going fine
Can I continue this interview when I've had another line?
Hello, I'm a model, I've got everything I need
How do I keep my figure? Well, that's down to speed.

Now I'm a best selling author, just an ordinary bloke
I get my best ideas with the little weed I smoke
Me, I'm an actor, a box office superstar
I like to go out drinking, propping up the bar.

I'm a presenter, you see me reading the news
But when I'm not on the box, I also drink lots of booze
Now me, I'm an 'It' girl, the talk of the town
You will find me in the toilet booting a line of brown

I'm a celebrity, TV got me fame
I have a chosen poison ... a few lines of cocaine
You know me, I'm a footballer, I play for England at the back
Last year I was in the papers, I got caught smoking crack

Now what keeps us together as we all unite as one?
We all got caught taking drugs but none of us got done.

So what sort of message does this send to people in the street?
To avoid drug convictions just change your name to Kate or Pete.

Shane Canning - HMP Highdown

I sleep in somebody's toilet

I sleep in somebody's toilet
In the bathtub I need to lie
Where the noise of taps drip, drip, drip
Plays a maddening lullaby
But sleeping in the lavatory
Has drawbacks, it's true
Especially when someone comes
And does a number two
For then the smell is unbearable
With the sound of plop, plop, plops
And a groan from the plopper
Pushing our faecal dollops
Here in my mattress placed in the bath
Where I'm forced to make my rest
Disturbed by the bowels of someone else
In this absurd sanitary nest

You read this with disbelief
You ask, 'How can this be?'
Why would anyone, why, why, why?
Live in a lavatory
But in a way this is no lie
In many ways it's true
For I share a cell in prison
And likewise share the loo
We eat, sleep and wash in here
As well as pee and crap
But with the smell of others faecal matter
It's enough to make you snap
So as I face another night
Think about my analogy
Would you sleep in the loo?
And deal with others scatology.

Ray Carrington - HMP Hull

Punishment, deterrent or just plain boring

Prison, jail, the slammer or the jug
Time and time I keep coming back, what a f**kin mug
But is this down to me not listening, or as my title suggests
Of all the ways of punishing me, is jail really the best?

It's the same old faces every time I come back to jail
As for most if they send you to jail they're setting you up to fail
Prolific offenders, habitual criminals, jails an occupational hazard
Just a rest till we get out and get f**kin bladdered

Open more jails, longer sentences I hear the government cry
But prison in its present state does not work, so I ask myself why?
Address people's drug problems, give them the help they need
Throw them in jail and they smoke smack not weed

Punishment, deterrent or just plain boring
Most prisoners stop in bed till dinner snoring
Up for dinner and then back on their bed
Go on a graft and get off their head

Prison is so wrong in so many ways
Cons just sit off and count down the days
Till release is here and they are homeward bound
Some think that that's it and everything's sound

But back again later on in the year
Either through women, drugs or beer
But as jails are it will never ever change
But people don't realise this and think that it's strange

So politicians, probation if you want jail to do its job
Spend some money, not just a few bob
Fifteen years in and out I have done, so there's living proof
Ask most prisoners and they'll tell you the truth

The reason why the prison population is soaring
It's neither a punishment or a deterrent, it's just plain boring

Paul Cartwright - HMP Liverpool

I'm innocent I tell you

I'm innocent I tell you please let me go
I'm innocent I tell you I just want you to know

I shouldn't be locked away behind this cell door
I'm innocent I tell you and I can't take no more

Over and over I pace across my pad
There's only so much I can take before I go mad

I shouldn't be here why can't no-one see
I don't belong here I should be out there and free

Soon I will be sentenced for something that I didn't even do
I was a suspect because I hung around in a bad crew

Never again will I come back to this hell
Never again will I have to stare at the walls of my cell

I hate this place I wish I could go home
But I know I can't I have to face this alone

Standing at my window listening to the girls talk
I hope when I go to court the judge says I can walk

I hope that he says go home and care for your mum
And don't let yourself become a jailbird bum

I hate the adult world it is so nasty and cruel
In here you have to obey every single rule

It's all yes boss no boss three bags full boss
No matter how much respect you show them they don't
   give a toss

It's all listen girl you're on your last warning
Now get behind your door we'll see you in the morning

So I go in and sit on my bed with my head in my hands
Twisting my fingers around my hair strands

Crying lonely tears right through the night
I am no longer strong enough to put up a fight

So I just leave the tears to run down my face
Please someone get me out of this place

Waiting every week for a razor and canteen
Having to have a morning strip wash so that I feel clean

I hate this place I just want to go home
I feel so depressed I feel so alone

I miss my mum and I miss my dad
I am fed up of feeling so sad

Well I don't think I'm getting out so I'll just do my time
I'll have to ride it out even though I didn't commit a crime

Rachel Charlton - HMP YOI Newhall

Living a lie

Four walls and a door
A ceiling and a solid cold floor
Shivering cold stuck in the system
A solid bronze mould their chipping
at the surfaces my soul starts to
erode, temper building I'm about to
explode the end result is violence
that I can't control, please sir open
the door I can't take it any more
A breath of fresh air a chance to stare
at the sky I finally realise that my
life is a lie it's time to repent my
sins this is the best chance I'll have
to start again. This is where the lie
stops and life begins.

Daniel Compton -
HMYOI Glen Parva

Happy 1st Birthday

Happy 1st Birthday my little one,
One year old today;
I should have shared this day with you
Instead of being away.

A year ago you blessed my life,
My beautiful little treasure;
You've brought such joy to every day
And I love you beyond measure.

I love to sit and watch you play
And crawl around the floor
And scramble to your little feet
And fall and rise once more.

I love to sit you on my lap
With a favourite book;
You're always so excited
You just can't wait to have a look.

I love your little noises
And the words you say
I love to watch all that you do
And see you learn every day.

You're such a happy little soul,
You bring smiles wherever you go;
You clap and wave those little hands
And people stop to say 'hello'.

I love to watch you in the bath
Playing with your toys
Your cow, your duck, your frog and fish
Or just splashing and making a noise.

When all is done at the end of the day,
I hold and cuddle you tight;
And I tell you how very special you are
Before I say 'goodnight'.

I watch and adore you as you sleep
Peaceful as can be;
And I wake in the morning to find you there
With a ready smile for me.

Happy birthday, again, my little one,
Have a lovely day;
I'll soon be back with you at home
And with you, I promise, I'll stay.

Bernadette Coote - HMP Bronzefield

What's it all for?

Hope is fading
The cage is near
Confinement calling
A fallen tear

Inevitable incarceration
Running its course
Nearly there now
Environment forced

Freedom gone now
Lost in the haze
Put on the mask
Enter the maze

Familiar place
Bring my head to this
So many faces
Not the ones I miss

The daily grind
Corroding the soul
A part of this place
The nightmare unfolds

One day ends
Another one loads
Repetition, monotony
My head explodes

Remembering freedom
Now so far away
Can't think too much
Can't let my mind stray

The futile waste
This daily war
Begging the question
What's it all for?

Anthony Corson - HMP
Liverpool

A Mother's Heartbreak

If those words you've written
Are honest and real
I'd have you back here
And not in a jail
My heart you have broken so many times
But I'll always love you despite all your crimes
You're loving and caring
As your mother I know
I can't wait for the day
You walk back through my door
There'll be tears in my eyes
And joy in my heart
But then I'll start wondering
Will the crimes start?
I've always stood by you whatever your mess
But no more can I take the pain and the stress
I'm sure you don't realise the things that you do
Of the pain that it causes to me, not to you
I sit and I wonder what's he doing today
And then I think back to our last holiday
I start to smile and then comes the tear
Oh I love you so much and I want you back here
I'm sat writing this and my heart it is broke
I've a lump in my throat and I'm starting to choke
I don't only love you I need you as well
Cos without you my son I'm going through hell
I try to be brave and I try not to cry
But when I come off a visit I just want to die
Because I can't hold you and make it all better
All we can do is talk through a letter
I keep on working just to pass time
Till you're in my arms and you've paid for your crime
No one can help me and I can't help you
Oh son what a pair, what are we gonna do?
I know that you love me, I know that you care
But I can't come to terms you're not here you're there
I've blamed myself from the day you were born
Cos I gave you life but to live it at home
You was always a good child
The best that I had, son was it my fault

➤

That you did something bad?
I come on a visit and I sit and I stare
I see my son sat in a prison chair
And then I wonder if I've steered you wrong
Cos then I should be punished and not my poor son
So with these words I'll leave you
Alone in your cell
And I'll go back to my own private hell
These words I speak Steven are honest and true
So remember your mother for life will love you.

From my heart to yours.

Denise Coulman

This poem was submitted by Steven Fethon, HMP Wolds. His mother wrote this poem to him in response to his poem called Broken Promises which he sent her after submitting it to Inside Time. He hopes that other readers will read this and realise how much their actions affect those that love them.

Da Concrete man

Did you hear about the man who grew from concrete
Proving nature's laws wrong.
The man truly DID, he grew from nothing
Funny it may seem. But by keeping its dreams
He learned to breathe fresh air.
Free at last, long live the man that grew from concrete.

Simon Crewe - HMP Lincoln

HMP Lincoln

As years went by in Lincoln prison the tension grew and grew
The inmate's protest got no response so what else could they do
The threats of grief was always there but no one knew the truth
Bad attitudes by all concerned cost Lincoln prison its roof
Year 2008 came, the summer dawned and then the day of fools
The day the prisoners went to pray with blades and wood for tools
The chaplain Proctor blessed these men with 'the Lord God be with you'
Then a voice rang out 'Now is the time' and they all knew what to do
Elation grew as they were given Lincoln on a plate
They swarmed the landings and opened cells saying I'm gonna find my mates
But many cons had other plans and wanted things they had seen
Like morphine in the pharmacy and tobacco from the canteen
The media came to stand and gloat and watch the prison burn
As hustlers soon got on to it as a chance to earn
While in the prison some heads got cracked and many minds got scarred
At sights of wrong ones getting slashed and kicked and beat with bars
But on the roof some lads had fun stood waving to their mates
Or picking screws hid below bombarding them with slates
For four long weeks the prisoners kept that prison under guard
With the sun above and the police below it really wasn't hard

And now in Lincoln with changes made and attitudes improved
The cons can see they made their point the day the system moved
But don't believe that all is well and happy ever after
For in jail you will often hear a wicked, evil laughter
That laughter comes within the night and chills you to the core
All the boys await the word 'Let's wreck the gaff once more'

Simon Crewe - HMP Lincoln

Loveless Weekend

Another loveless weekend
And its my own fault I'm alone
I toss and turn in the dark
Feeling pain I've never known

Just outside my window
There's a full moon in the sky
Every leaf is dancing
As the winds of night pass by

There's sorrow in my heart
And a tear in my eye
First one, then another
Till my pillow is no longer dry

I took your love for granted
Putting your needs on the shelf
Feasting on all you gave
Only thinking of myself

Then God sent you another
To reward the person you are
Someone who would love you
At home and afar

Seeking your approval
By how they use their mind
Always speaking words of truth
Preferring to be kind

To your memory I confess
For I no longer have your ear
I pray for God's forgiveness
And for love beyond my tear

Paul Crewe - HMYOI Hindley

The Special Brew Crew

2-4-5-8 make it a crate
A slab of 24 cans of special brew mate
A can of brew for breakfast 'n' I feel great
24 cans later, I'm in aright 2 and 8
You know all I want to do if the truth be told
Is hang around outside drinkin' Carlsberg liquid gold
To maximise the pleasure it should always be drank cold
And if I've been munching Es, I always drink untold
Ecstasy and special brew is such a wicked buzz
Nor sure how or why – I don't know what it does
But every time I mix 'em I get in trouble with the fuzz
Why do the bloody filth always seem to harass us
No drinkin' in public places is such a fucked up law
What do they think park benches and cans of beer are for?
It gives the filth a kick to pour my beer onto the floor
And say don't let me catch you drinking brew round here no more
But when the brew crews out in force they don't come near
They tip toe past in silence trembling with fear
We'd kick their fuckin' heads in the situations clear
Don't ever come between the special brew crew and their beer
Why such fascist laws, why can't I get pissed in peace?
Special brew's expensive without fines from the police
If the coppers were drunk too, we'd all get along with ease
We'd stagger round as drunk as lords drinkin' where we pleased

Harry Cross - HMP Lewes

A Decision

Every day a different decision,
A decision every day and night.

One day I made a decision that changed my life,
It has caused me to be all alone,
In a tiny cell which is now my home.

With no one but me,
My life is ruled by officers and their keys.

If only that day I had made the decision to go somewhere else.
My life now would not be in such a mess.

Now I wait patiently for my trial,
I have to stand up,
Head held high,
To speak no lies.

Every day until then I will do nothing but cry,
Because this was my decision,
What will be is my fate.

Prudence Crouch – HMP Bronzefield

Red Head

If only I could remember your number I'd give you a call.
I know it starts off 075 but I can't remember the rest at all.
Just to see you, smell you, kiss your lips, I remember the last time I saw you.
The last time we were together and you left, swinging your hips.

Your natural red hair blowing in the breeze,
A voice in the back of my mind said you're such a tease.
It's one of the attractions the reason I gave you my number.
That day we met that day I can't forget.

I guess you're pissed off with me, thinking I'm blanking your calls.
If only you knew, No not at all how much I miss you now.
See I've got that earring you've been asking for.
I found it back at mine, when I was cleaning the floor.

I swear when I get out of here I will return your earring no worries dear.
I'll even buy you new ones yes a new pair, when I get out of here.
You probably threw the other in the bin.
If I'm lucky I'll turn that earring into a big diamond ring

So do not forget me or cast me aside.
Keep dreaming red head deep the dream alive.

Mr Curtis - HMP Wandsworth

Same old shit ... just another day

Why do I have to wake in da morning
To da same old shit it's very boring
Da same old screws and same old cons
Facing up to all our wrongs.
Same old slop and same routines
Oil on bread and uncooked beans
Waiting all day just for a letter
Hoping that next day will be better.
Same old boys and same old tramps
"Got any burn, I'll swap you some stamps"
Snooping screws from cell to cell
After phones dat they can sell.
Snorting subbies and smoking gear
Dis goes on from year to year
When will they ever realise
It's just to disguise our destructive lives.
You get a nicking and go down da block
Little did they know your burn is in your sock
All these words 'aint no lies
You'll hear it from all da other guys.
'I've done this' and 'I've done that'
Everyone thinks they're da biggest cat
On da yard you hear them cry
How they done this and why.
It's always da same on exercise
Same old shit and same old lies
Same old boys waiting for parcels
It doesn't come over - 'fucking arseholes'.
Over it comes you hear it land
What a throw just as planned
Screws come running from left to right
By da time they get close it's out of sight.
In we go having a laugh and a joke
Hurrying up so we can have a smoke
You put in an app to get enhanced
You hear da same shit, 'you got no chance'.
Don't forget cos this is true
All this bullshit is down to you
It's always da same in every way
Same old shit ... just another day.

Martyn Dance & Marc Harris - HMP Bristol

Prison Officer

Why do you talk to me
Like I'm dirt on your shoe?
I am a human being too
Your harshness cuts me like a knife
I can't take much more of this life!

Why treat me like I'm someone you hate?
You have a job to do this I appreciate,
But can't we just try to get along?
Is what I'm asking really so wrong?

We're not so different you and me
You could be on this side of the fence too
I know I've committed a dreadful crime
But please leave me alone to do my time.

Stop trying to bully me to leave your mark
Even though you say your bites
Worse than your bark
Your words really hurt me, it's no lie
They make me want to curl up and die!

Lisa Marie Davies - HMP Send

First Kiss

Meet me at eight-thirty, surreptitiously
We can't let slip our feelings, inadvertently
Our hearts solitude has gone on extensively
It's time to release this grief, it's so costly
As I approach the fateful meeting, apprehensively
I feel a strange euphoria welling up in me
I call you on the phone to ask audaciously
If I can steal a kiss, most passionately
Yes! Yes! Yes! You answer, excitedly
I thought you would never ask it of me
I drop down from my chariot, impatiently
How about my kiss then? I ask anxiously
Are you sure you're ready for what might be?
No, but are any of us ready for eternity?
I don't suppose we are, come here then kiss me
This is the feeling I've searched for, tirelessly
Two people loving each other, unconditionally
Unfortunately I have to leave you momentarily
But I'll return, most definitely
Now I've found my one true love
Serendipitously

Richard Davison - HMP Elmley

Shell Shocked

I may not be in a battlefield
In a military sense
I haven't used a firearm
Or lived inside a trench
Reading touching letters
Sent by the ones I love
Or diving from the terror
In the skies above
But all the fear that lingers
Once they leave that hell
Will compare quite closely
To when I leave my cell
Pain that's felt unjustly
At someone else's command
Innocent or guilty?
Broken is what I am

Adam Dellicott -
HMP Birmingham

Incarceration:
The Nature of the Beast
(Penance & Purgatory)

Unrelenting, unforgiving, contemptuous and taciturn,
Dangerous dominator, unseen usurper,
Cruel to be kind and kind to be cruel,
Twisted sobriety, lacklustre and belligerent,
Penance and servitude in the belly of the beast.

Cumbersome, loathsome, savage, dark,
Struggling, striving, ducking and diving,
Cunning, conniving, misery thriving,
Alone in purgatory, den of iniquity,
Creature of habit, deficient, void of feeling.

Vexatious to the spirit, destroyer of the soul,
Degradingly derisive, tormenting torturer,
Sycophantic serpent, unsophisticated qualifier,
Unrequited muse, accomplished liar,
Anarchic recidivist, wallflower of mire.

Burgeoning, beguiling, iconoclastically demure,
Disaffected, defunct, deranged and deluded,
Never gaining, ever losing, amoral, corrupt,
Socially excluded like a fork tongued pariah,
Ostracised, nomadic, consequential and dire.

Impetuous and brash, unashamedly daring,
Emotionally crippled, vaguely uncaring,
Indecision, obsession, complexity of mind,
Callous, uncouth, cold and uncompromising,
This, my friend, is The Nature of the Beast!

Ian Dickens - HMP Gartree

Nothing is ever lost

The trees tower above the lifeless grey prison wall
I witness the transition from summer to fall
Leaves once green wrinkle, die and turn brown,
Forever they fall down, forever down.

This cell is my own doing, my own private hell,
Try as I might but there is no one to tell,
To tell of my troubles, fears and woes,
A friend once said, ce sera so life goes.

Like the leaves I hold on with all of my might,
I can't help but think I will lose this fight,
However, we must persevere and hold on for one more day,
Summer comes and goes but the good times
Are in our memories to stay.

Shane Dobson - HMP Hull

The Voice

Where does it come from
Nobody knows,
It has great powers from the unknown.
My brain it talks to me, its name is Frank
He orders me about like a little boy scout.
He sounds so real, even though it is not,
This voice in my head can go and rot!
There's this little blue pill that can make it go away,
Then it's like a child who's frightened to go out and play.
It commands I do its bidding by hurting myself.
Sometimes it winds, as my arms are a mess,
But it's getting quieter now,
At last the blue pill has kicked in.
So for now I will hear you later,
You devil within
It will not beat me, because I'm stronger than him.

Jason Dobson - HMP Shrewsbury

Nike Air Max and Flip Flops

Football, snooker and Sky TV
This is what prison means to me,
Three meals a day with coffee or tea
Better than cheap, it's provided free.
With joggers, jumpers and shoes
Laundered whenever you choose,
Daily papers for the morning news
Go sell smack coz you can't lose.
College, Chapel and gym
Books, barbells and hymns,
Seven days a week you win
Away from the temptations of sin.
Low paid hours and hairy showers
Crack heads, bullies and chicken shit liars,
Double or nothing betting schemes
A rollie for a pack of bourbon creams.
Butchered haircuts on macho men
Brew packs, Mars bars and biro pens,
Grafted Y-fronts and recorded calls
Toothpaste and bogeys on the walls.
Black slippers, black pants, white socks
Scraggy beards and bald spots,
Dressing gowns and vests
Nike Air Max and Flip-Flops.

Randy Donegan - HMP Altcourse

Repentance

Sorry was so hard to say
It's a word I think of now everyday
Before that came an attitude change
Inside my head the emotions range
Admission of crime
For which I do time
A hard look in the mirror to see the wrongs
Retributive justice for a coked up con
History can't have a rewrite
But even now I refuse my pipe
Enough of the drugs to numb the pain
I finally face what drove me insane
Now I'm here I'll try my best
So I'm not written off like the rest
Of my past I'm fully shamed
My inner demons I have to tame
Remorse, regret full of sorrows
A new start, my hope of tomorrow.

Shama Dookhooah - HMP Downview

Fish A Wish

Wishing just for wishing sake
Is fishing in an empty lake
Yet ignorance of lack of fish
Can make us stay to wish and wish

Fates to fish in a teeming lake
With line and hook but lack of bait
You may not leave with loaded net
But chances are a fish you'll get

This may not be the fish you sought
But use it well the thing you've caught
For put to line and to lake returned
With each new catch new thing is earned

Iain Doyle - HMP Preston

What's special about Special Brew?

I just had to write in reply to the Special Brew Crew
To let people know the trouble that stuff got me into
And boy did I ever pay the price
For drinking a lager that tasted so nice.

We'd call it the Devil's potion or fizzy whiskey
Whatever it's made with it just sends you crazy
One or two cans and things would be all right
But four, five or more and it would always end up in a fight

And add to that buzz we would have a puff
Feel bulletproof and tougher than tough
Don't fuck with us when we feel like this
Not the Special Brew Crew whose on the piss

If you do then just be warned
Exactly what the Devil has spawned!
We're braver than Braveheart, more nuts than KP
But also more reckless and as stupid as can be

This drink brings out a person that just isn't me
But one dark night things went just too far
For no justifiable reason, I attacked a man with a metal bar
I didn't know until the next day that I'd cracked open his head

And the resulting injuries had left this man dead
It wasn't my intention to harm this man
But all of my actions came from the Brew can
Twenty two years later I'm still in prison, still paying the price
Did I really say that Special Brew tasted so NICE!!

So, advice to those for the next time they drink
Please stop and have a think!
It may not be your intention to harm or maim
But what happened to me could happen again – to you.

CARLSBERG SPECIAL BREW
PROBABLY THE MOST DANGEROUS LAGER IN THE WORLD

Will Draven - SE London

I wrote some words reflecting my experience and the consequences of drinking. I hope somewhere in these words there will be people who will heed the warning of the dangers and consequences of drinking.

In the dock

Not guilty said I : A pervert he said,
A human am I : An animal instead,
A poet I claim : A deviant in law,
With words I paint : With words you score,
A family man : A risk to us all,
I share love and warmth : What you are is The Fall,
A walk with the dog : A walk with a screw;
I am freedom : Take him down!

DSMS - HMP Usk

Memories

Each and every day when others are asleep
I take a trip down memory lane with a tear upon my cheek
I cry because I love you
I cry because I care
I cry because when I awake I know you won't be there
Love is like a feather
But you'll end up with me forever and ever

Jaheer Duel - HMP Brixton

A changed man

Close the door and turn the key
Nobody in here cares about me
Leave me here on my own
My heart is saying 'I want to go home'
In the morning when I wake up
I'll drink the coffee from a plastic cup
Off to work, my trousers are green
People look scary and some look mean
Working away I feel so down
'what you staring at' I say with a frown
He then stands up and clenches his fists
My temper rises, I see green mist
He starts to shout at the top of his voice
I have to fight, I've got no choice
The fists then fly to each others nose
Who will win, nobody knows
The alarm is pressed, screws run through
    the door
You better hurry up, he is on the floor
I lost my temper I don't know why
I'm usually quiet and sometimes shy
Off I'm dragged still tense as a rock
Not to my cell but down the block
My breath is short I feel so mad
This isn't me, I'm not all bad
Look what it's doing, this place called jail
I want to succeed, not to fail
I want to do the best I can
Can it change me? ... Yes it can!

Jamie Dunning - HMP Ashwell

Institutionalization

World's gone and got itself
In a big damn hurry
I falter and hesitate
At zebra crossings
Stop, wait, walk, stop, wait, walk
Too late, what's up with these people
Why don't they slow down
Hearty laughter fills the bar
I join in
It doesn't come out proper
Knowing eyes bore into me
I've been found out
Conversations overlap
And
Merge into one another
Unintelligible
Buzzing
Droning
Like a dream sequence
Stepping outside the moment
Looking back in
Like a peeping Tom
At Christmas time
Through a snow frosted window
Hazy happy faces
Vibrant rosy complexions
Animated
Gesticulating wildly
Freedom
I don't belong here
Doctor Spock
Energize
Yes
That is a Yale key alright
I've seen them before
Solid brass
I open the door
High ceilings
Huge bay windows
Furniture re-arranged
Pulled
Slowly but surely
Into the middle
Of the room
Like an open plan cell
I was home

Paul Eaton - HMP Bristol

I wonder

I wonder why my eyes no longer cry
The way they did the day you went away,
The day you took the sun out of the sky
And made my life a thousand shades of grey.

I wonder why my heart no longer aches
When photographs remind me of your smile,
Or some forgotten memory awakes
And urges me to linger for a while.

I wonder why the garden where we kissed
Is overgrown and withered with neglect,
A place that time has shrouded in the mist
That clouds my eyes whenever I reflect.

I wonder why the letters that you wrote
Have faded now like roses left to die,
The scent of love that kept my hopes afloat
Has vanished like the tears I used to cry.

I wonder why the wind still calls your name
And haunts me like an old familiar rhyme;
Why love alone has kept alive the flame
That flickers through the corridors of time.

I wonder at the closing of the day
Why thoughts of you still follow me to sleep,
And though my eyes still keep the tears at bay,
I know my lonely heart will always weep.

Tony Edwards - HMP Camp Hill

Legacy

Like vampires with a thirst for blood
You terrorise the neighbourhood
And feed upon the fear,
But such aggression wields a price,
So listen to this sound advice:
The price you pay is dear.

The legacy you leave behind,
As men of violence, men unkind,
Will stigmatise your kids;
For them the sun will never shine
Because their dads were Frankenstein,
Immoral invalids.

A child will take his father's lead
And emulate his every deed
To stir his father's pride
And years from now when he has grown
And teaches children of his own
Their morals will subside.

And they, the kids of violent men
Will deal in violence once again,
Perpetuate the trends;
And so it goes, from dad to son,
The legacy goes on and on,
The violence never ends.

Tony Edwards - HMP Camp Hill

Marbles

Please help me find my marbles,
I don't know where they are,
I left them in an ashtray
Full of nicotine and tar.
They rattled their objection
As I sucked upon a fag,
Succumbing to infection
As my lungs began to gag.
I left them in a cloud of smoke
While cancer filled the air,
They died when I began to choke,
Though I was unaware.
My marbles now are scrambled,
I'm feeling so confused,
With nicotine I gambled,
My health I self-abused.

Tony Edwards -
HMP Camp Hill

Taking The Piss

It started back in ninety five
When Tories struggled to survive
And show they had some balls;
In order to increase arrests
They introduced compulsory tests
Within all prison walls

The plan that Michael Howard devised
Was very cleverly disguised
To mask its true intent:
If heroin could be employed
To render felons stupefied
Then no one would lament.

The way in which it was achieved
Would mean the public were deceived
And they would bear the brunt
For crime would quickly escalate
As addicts left each prison gate
Their drug of choice to hunt.

When cannabis was in the air
It tranquillised the dark despair
That lurks in every cell;
It gave the blues a place to hide
And banished thoughts of suicide
When cons were close to Hell

But when the piss test came along
Resentment on the wings was strong
For cons were losing time:
A spliff was costing fourteen days
Which punished in all sorts of ways
For this horrendous crime

A drug that in the system stays
For weeks and weeks instead of days
Is easy to detect
So those who used to build a spliff
All turned to smack and coke to sniff
And some they did inject

➤

In time the dragon takes its toll
As it corrupts the heart and soul
Of those who are naive;
For harmless spliffs are cast aside
By those who sacrifice their pride
Their loved ones to deceive

And when their discharge comes around
Their state of mind no longer sound
Heroin addicted
The only thought inside their brain
Is, buy a bag to ease the pain
A habit self-inflicted

And when that tiny bag has gone
Their habit just goes on and on
So they resort to crime
If this is what the State intended
Can piss tests ever be defended
Today or any time?

Tony Edwards - HMP Camp Hill

Institutionalised

Dreary, misery my life has become
This oppressive cage
Is too much to overcome
My life has become a deja vu
Broken only by my rendezvous
The visits they serve mostly to tease
My yearning for freedom
They do not appease
I'm trapped in a cage
Please acknowledge my rage
This chapter is foreign
It's not part of my page
They tell me behaviour shows maturity
I tell them compliance shows docility
I refuse to conform
So they call me insubordinate
Then put me on basic
I refuse to co-operate
I'm living in hell
What more can I say
A minute is an hour
And a month is a day
No, the reverse in fact
A day is a month
I rely on my will
But it's barely enough
I'm going insane
I'm losing my mind
So I go to the gym
To help me unwind
My release is at hand
But yet it's afraid
So restless I stay
Till my departure's fulfilled
So soon I'll be gone
Away from this hole
But the constant oppression
Is taking it's toll
But soon I'll be out
On the menacing streets

With faces unknown
Just me on my own
No friends or foes
No uniformed clothes
No keys, no locks
No wings, no blocks
Just cars and roads
Civilians, pedestrians
They're all out to get me
Police and judges
They all want to hurt me
They hate me I tell you
Save me I implore you
Leave me in here
Away from their glares
I can't go out
The world is a mystery
In here I'm a legend
I'm part of the history
In here I'm respected
Out there I'm insulted
Out there I'm a nuisance
In here I'm exalted
This is my home
Finally I realise
I can't go back
I've been institutionalised!

Osaleni Eubuomwan -
HMP YOI Rochester

Round and round we go!!

Breaking the circle has always been the problem for me,
Released from prison without a care, once again I'm set free,
Goals, ambitions, achievements, people to see and places to be,
Self-will keeps me going, tooing and throwing, no drugs, no drink,
Just plenty of gym and plenty of time to think.
Old faces and triggers always a reminder calling my name,
A moment of weakness, a pint, a fag, I look for something to blame,
Regrets turn to anger, self pity but most of all shame,
It happens again and again, then something happens and I'm full of pain,
Here we go I tell myself, not knowing when to stop,
Dishonesty and drugs, lies and crime, even my sex life becomes a flop.
Isolating myself from family and true friends,
Black boxed cars and warehouse alarm bells ringing as the crowbar bends,
Manipulation, blagging and borrowing as I know the time's coming,
Police chases, house raids I know the place where I'm going,
A trail of destruction until the day I'm finally caught,
Handcuffs, no bail just straight to jail without a thought,
Apologies, letters and phone calls to make amends,
Visits and plenty of gym to look good for family and friends,
A few courses and some self belief is all I have to show,
Not long until release,
Round and round we go …

Tony Evans - HMP Bullingdon
A story of me and my addiction and the circle I'm trying to break

When Heroin Brings You To Your Knees

When heroin brings you to your knees
You don't see butterflies
Birds or bees
The scent of flowers
A distant thought
The breeze through trees
Is soon forgot
This is what you do not see
When heroin brings you to your knees

When heroin brings you to your knees
Love's forgot
Souls start to freeze
Not feeling happiness
Nor feeling pain
Inside your mind
Feels numbed/insane
When you have no-one
Left to please
Heroin's brought you to your knees

Now that you're clean
And standing tall
You see the autumn leaves
That fall
You smell the air and feel the breeze
Birds are singing
In the trees
The sky is bright
The world is yours
You soon fall down
Land on all fours
Everything you've lost
And loved
Never ever
Was worth the cost
Now your eyes are open
Full of tears
How could I have lost
So many years
By heroin bringing me to my knees

The Drug
The Bug
The Addict
The Mug

James Farricker - HMP Birmingham

My life

There's a life outside that's waiting for me
A life full of hope
A life not yet crushed by these cell walls
A life that's anxious for me to return
And take my rightful place
Among the branches of the tree of life,
My life.
This life that I am surrounded by
Is the only reality of now
Not ever
Not forever
And though it's true what they say
You can find the best friends you'll ever have in prison
These are not the people I've chosen to be with
These are not the people I call my own
They are not from my home.

There's a life outside that's waiting for me
It's full of colours and smells and tastes
It's full of fresh new mornings
It's full of dreams in the process of being fulfilled
It's day after new day of attachments and attractions
And of brand new shoes
Shoes that I choose
This reality of now
Is not forever
It's a past waiting to be looked back upon
To reflect upon in moments of quiet
It is a pause in the sentence of my story
In the beginning I thought it was my end
But in the end, it was my beginning.

There is a life outside
And it's waiting for me
It's sitting there tapping its feet, patiently
It sounds like my son's voice
Giggling with pleasure
It smells of fresh air and exotic perfume
It tastes like cherries and mangoes and home cooked spaghetti Bolognese
It looks like the greenest grass
And the bluest sky
Not the sky framed by the rogues gallery of HMP Bronzefield
But **my** sky
And it feels
It feels like **my** freedom
My life and **my** dreams
And it's waiting for me
It's my reality

Alma Fekete - HMP Peterborough

Rip Offs

Aramark suppliers have you no shame
Ripping us all off, what's your bloody game?

We are a captive audience to that we're all aware
So stop ripping us all off, it's really not that fair

Let Asda take on Aramark for the prices they'll compete
Instead of charging us over the odds, treating us like scum on their feet

We all think what you're doing is not that nice
Because outside we know we'll get it half the price

We've all been punished for our crimes and ended up in the dock
So why do you advertise things, what aren't even in stock

Why won't you change our faulty goods straight away
Is it because we're in prison and here to stay

We've no leg to stand on, if we open our canteen bags
So why send us dry bacci for rolling our fags

All the prices you have put up are obviously the best sellers
That's also my opinion and every other fellas

You already know why we complain and moan
It's because we're charged seven times more, for using a prison phone

You may have gave a lot to Children in Need
But was that to disguise the corruption and greed

Steven Fethon - HMP Wolds

Déja vu

I land in reception
No way three years
It was only fraud and deception

E're mate sort us a smoke
Yeah no probs
Av ya got any dope
I start to laugh
What's so funny it wasn't a joke

Ey mate wot's it saying in ere?
It's ok
Three on sir

Boss where's my burn
I've rang the bell
My stomach starts to churn
Are you taking the piss son?
Nah, just want my burn

The door opens, same old faces
Only this time I've filled one of their places
The landings are loud
And what's with the crowd
Someone's scrapping, nothings changed
And not much happening

I've got an hour
Then it's back behind my door
It's like déja vu
I've been here before

Right lad time for induction
Gym, chapel, then to the main store

Back on the wing
Same cleaner from last time still
Mopping the floor
Door's slamming shut
And screws on the mooch
Shit I'd better go move that hooch

Time goes by so quickly
Before I know it I'm out the gate
Few bevies with the lads
Shit my curfew I'm late

The door comes in
For God's sake don't the old bill give in
You've been recalled lad
Jesus, I was only late by a min

Then once again I'm being driven
Through the gate
Same year
Same place
And back to my same old mates

Jonny Fowler - HMP Lindholme

I Miss Momma

Man, I miss my momma …
I cried alone when she died
I really cried
(it was two years ago)
As hard and tough as I am,
I can't lie
About the day my momma's life was denied
I miss my momma …

Sometimes when I'm alone in my mind
And think of past years
Sweat rolls down my face
And blends in with my tears,
Nobody but myself to blame
For broken promises,
At least now, I know heaven's where my momma is
I miss my momma …

The day that she died
I was stuck in a prison cell
A bottomless well, the hottest hell,
(I couldn't breathe) not very well
I couldn't talk, I couldn't hear, I couldn't see,
The day my momma left me,
My thoughts were joy, mixed with misery
I miss my momma …

I think about my momma
Every single day
Sometimes I hear her yelling at me,
Sometimes I hear her pray,
I wish I had been a better son
But as far as mothers go,
She was my only one
I miss my momma …

So, if your momma is still in this world,
Treat her like she's your favourite girl,
If you focus on her faults and her blemishes
It will only ensure
That love diminishes,
And when she's gone –
You'll miss your momma.

Brian Franklin Thames -
Centinela State Prison USA

Billie Basic!

I'm locked here behind my door
Oh my God, what a bore
I'm sat here with nothing at all
Not even a tele or clock on the wall
You may be able to lock the locks
But they will never stop them clocks
One day I will be back home
Back to the streets I used to roam

You said to me basic for a week
It's been ten days, oh you geek
Why don't you just do my review
Cos let's face it, it won't hurt you

I get an hour a day to go for a mooch
But while I'm in I'm brewing hooch
Got no toiletries I've traded them all
Subutex has been my downfall
I sit here and gouch to death
That's off Subbies not the meth

The Subutex will soon be dry
Then I'll do my rip and cry
But don't you worry about me
I'll soon get back my TV
I'll just sit here and chill to Cascada
UB40 or maybe Nevada

Tracie Frost - HMP Styal

Freedom

Freedom the backbone of a democratic nation
Freedom to roam this imperial creation
Freedom said they Bush and Blair with their ideas
Freedom to walk these streets full of spies
Freedom, freedom democracy, meritocracy, hypocrisy
Freedom freedom land of the brave, countries of war
    blood on floor
Freedom freedom democracy will prevail
Freedom's sending your citizens to jail
Freedom from them who hide behind a wall
Freedom under the guise of the Christian call
Whilst their bombs their ideology needs to look at itself
4,000 Americans all dead for their wealth
Soldiers that die for freedom's sake
Mothers that cry politicians act fake
Their bombs their cause a chapter of death
Tell that to a soldier who gasps his last breath
Securing such freedom from violence to calm
Freedom's alarm who blames from the arm
One love one dream one heart one soul
One flagrant dream of mind's control
Freedom, freedom what price will we pay
Surreptitiously planning to plunder take away
Violence the lost bastion of moral cowardice
Peace the will of all good men
Freedom of choice freedom of speech freedom of minds
Freedom to live freedom to die freedom while Bush
    watches babies cry
Democracy and its hypocrisy. But think about this
Are we ever really free to live our lives in harmony?

Mathew Gallagher - HMP Parkhurst

Mum

So many times I've asked myself
Why do you trouble so
You struggle with the chores of life
And wander to and fro
Why can't you take things easy
And take life in its pace
And brush away that worried look
From your tender loving face
Don't worry about tomorrow
Think about today
You cannot put the world to rights
With thoughts of yesterday
Think about yourself for once
And give yourself a break
Dear mum of mine you are the best
You give but you don't take
I've often heard you crying
I've often heard you sigh
I've often heard the way you ask
God's help to get you by
I'm sure the Lord can hear you
I'm sure he knows the way
I'm sure he will remember you
Upon your judgement day
He'll put his arms around you
And dry away your tears
And walk you through the Promised Land
No heartache and no fears.

M Gibbons - HMP Manchester

The Greedy Bankers

So the Greedy Bankers have had their fill
Just as Marx said they always will
Now it's gone pear shape
They've left it to the taxpayer
While they jet off to places like Marbella

The Greedy Bankers have left the country broke,
To them it's all a joke
The Government bail them out every time
So the Greedy Bankers love their sub prime
Regardless of whether people could afford it
The Greedy Bankers tried to squeeze every last bit
'Why rent when you can buy?' they chanted
'Poor credit history? No problem, mortgage granted!'

Now it's blown up in their face
And shown they really are a disgrace

Their dirty little secret has now come to light
And suddenly, they've got rather tight
They've all but stopped lending money
Which is rather funny
"Cos the irony is it's all their fault
With all the bad debt they bought

Surely this shows capitalism is flawed
And the Greedy Bankers are universally abhorred

Daniel Goldsmith - HMP Gartree

Rewind

Peacefully sitting in the evening sun,
The wind's gentle breeze caressing me,
All maelstroms now confined to history,
They are well documented, once so central to my life,
Troubled times are now just a distance memory,
In my twilight years I have peace, I sleep well.
Sitting alone I contemplate,
Rewinding through my history, revisiting my life,
Thoughts of children so happy in their ways,
They are older now, a part of me in them.
I am content; I have lived a full life.
Friends I have made and friends I have lost,
Always a cost when you breathe,
This is life; it's over before it begins
That is my life; a moment in time,
Toiling so hard in the fields of humanity,
Now I rest. I have earned that right.
At night I watch the stars and look for moon dust,
Retracing my steps I float above the clouds,
At times so clumsy, yet such fun.
I rewind.
It is intoxicating, I drink it all, exhilarated by the replays,
But I remain sober, maturity is mine now.
The sandman returns, he has friends with him,
Friends I do not know, they are early,
I ask them to leave.
A knock at my door, I smile,
Someone calls my name, the voice so innocent, so pure,
It calls to me like a songbird,
'Grandpa are you in?' 'Yes I am in.'
We sit in the evening sun and exchange silly stories.
Then he is gone.
Alone again.
I rewind.

Robert Gray - HMP Maidstone

The Harvest

I look from within this darkened place
No seasons here, just disgrace
Images forming in my mind
Another place, another time
The gathering of the ripened crops
The cooling breeze, I soon forgot
Late maturity with slow decline
Autumnal beauty, for me to find
Sculptured fields of barley, maize
Vibrant in the autumn haze
Idyllic thoughts, picturesque scenes
Caressing all of nature's dreams
The harvester cut his path so deep
Fallow I lie, and now I sleep

Robert Gray - HMP Maidstone

Waiting

Here I sit, alone in my world
I hold a magic lantern
Waiting... waiting
For Saint Bernard to arrive

I watch the Machiavellian machinists
They work tirelessly, never stopping
Unscrupulous in their ways
Their cold heartiness rules my life

I oscillate between worlds
Such contrasts ... they wait
This life in an iron lung
So futile ... I wait

There must be an irony here
But I'm too blind to see, too far gone
Geriatric people, time worn, lizard like
Shuffling along in the land of the ostrich

Late at night when all is quiet
My lantern glows, I can feel its warmth
Through the crack in the glass I can see ... my future ... or is it my past?

Dignified people think of me
They are waiting ... waiting
They share in my pain
They are waiting ... just waiting

Robert Gray - HMP Maidstone

The way it was

So loyal I stay,
A Beretta in my hand ready to go,
Run in a bank everything seems slow,
My boys beside me shouting as well,
The people in the bank have just tasted hell,
Bagged the money a minute has passed,
Need to get out,
Out so fast.

Two weeks later I'm in my bed,
Armed response with a gun to my head,
Just woke up,
What can I do,
Best stay still for the boys in blue.

At the cop shop they say to me,
There was more than you,
There was three,
I look at them with hate in my eyes
    and a frown on my face,
To me the cops are just a disgrace,
I got no comment all the way,
I was born a bad boy,
So loyal I stay.

I stand in the dock,
I stand all alone,
With pride in my eyes,
Because my boys are at home.

The judge looked at me and said lock him away,
Until he comes back to reach judgement day.

A few months later I'm back in the dock,
I'm looking at the judge,
He's looking at the clock,
To my freedom he now holds the key,
He must be bored with lads like me,
Now he has me in his sight,
With words so harsh he gives me a fright,
A reality check,
It comes as a blow,
Off to jail,
I must go.

Nathan Greef - HMP Brixton

Try me sometime

I quietly admired her from afar
Perfectly perfect behind the bar
Two pints of Stella and some peanuts please love
And while you're at it give that dickhead the shove

Come be with me, I'll take you away
I might even take you to Egypt one day
She gave me that smile that said 'Don't push
it mate, I took you to bed but I don't want a date'

'Last night was amazing' she said via text,
Not 'marry me', 'love ya' or 'when can we meet next'
I guess I'll just leave it I thought in my head
If she's happy I'm happy my heart sank like lead

Leave her alone? Easier said than done
I don't quite yet love her but she could be the one!
It's not meant to guilt you, my five minute rhyme
It's only to ask you just try me sometime

Steen Grundy - HMP Parc

Dedicated to Buttons a very special young lady in my life.

Life sentence

Three score years and ten were handed down
A span at first too long to comprehend,
I lay and cried, in tears I seemed to drown,
Locked in behind my bars without a friend;
A visitor transformed my lonely space –
I looked into my mother's smiling face.

The passing years brought yearnings to be free
But borders etched with love kept me confined,
And teachers were like gaolers but taught me
To scale the walls of ignorance and find
The precious freedom that true learning brings;
The journeys of the mind's imaginings.

Full grown, we enter freedom's path; it seems
Unsigned, our journey started joyfully
May lead to cul-de-sacs of thwarted dreams
Or to the anxious, halting times when we,
Trapped by our inhibitions, cease to strive;
Such are the many prisons we survive.

Our term near spent, we will become, too fast,
A captive of the body's fading strength,
Escape is the remembrance of joys past
Till blind night's darkness shifts our thoughts at length
Towards an undiscovered country's peace,
The almost wanted, almost feared release.

One winter's day, the black crows overhead
Survey the muffled mourners; frozen clay
Will clasp the coffin'd husk that I have shed,
While I, released, escape this pain-filled, gay,
Enchanted place, my time here served, I go;
The final freedom all of us will know.

Keith Hall - HMP Springhill

Sunday Best

On empty Sunday pavements, sanctified
By banishment of work bound feet, I ride
My junior bike, with father's guiding hand,
To Sunday school, with polished features and
In Sunday best.

The five year-old - my long lost self - released
Angelic countenance to trusted priest,
And after bible story closed I took
My storied stamp, to glue in Sunday book
With reverence.

But grown up journeys veered from sacred ways,
I found no guiding hand in life's sad maze,
And soon I'll face, no longer at my best,
The longest journey of my life – undressed
And unencumbered.

No stained glass stamps or priestly certainty
Will join me on that void embracing sea;
Was childhood's pure and simple faith not true?
But if a Listener waits: I tried to do
My Sunday best.

Keith Hall - HMP Springhill

Shhhhh

Through the sound of voices chattering, be silent
Through the sound of traffic murmuring, be silent
Through the sound of people constructing buildings, be silent
Through the sound of televisions and radios, be silent

In the sound of wind blowing, listen
In the sounds of birds singing, listen
In the sound running water, listen
In the sound of breathing, listen
In the thoughts of your mind, listen
In the depths of your soul, listen

Listen!

Stuart Hall - HMP Parkhurst

If only

Once upon when I was free
There was a man who held a key
He opened up a door for me
He let me see what I could be

When I saw what I could see
I didn't like what I could be
I didn't like what I could see
I didn't wanna be that me

So I asked that man who held the key
Can I change what I can see
Can I change what I can be
Can I be another me
And can I please have that key
Cos all I wanna be is free

That man he turned and said to me
That is not what has to be
You can change what you can see
You have a choice what is to be
All you have to do is see

The key is not what sets you free
Only you can set you free

Once upon when I was free
There was a man who held a key
He opened up a door for me
He let me see what I could be

Dean Hamilton –
HMP Featherstone

Living InThis Grave

I see cemented places
As I make my merry way
I meet demented faces
Each and every day
I walk among these masses
I smile, I nod, I wave
How slow time it passes
While I'm living in this grave

Dean Hamilton -
HMP Featherstone

Drinking then jail

Since I turned eighteen, I've been heavy drinking,
I've done naughty things, without even thinking,
And people did tell me, I'd end up in prison,
But I didn't care and I didn't listen.

Then one day it happened, I didn't get bail,
Got cuffed in the dock, and then taken to jail,
Remanded for two weeks, then back up in court,
'I'll get a long sentence', well that's what I thought.

Got lucky the first time and walked free that day,
'I'll stay out of trouble', is what I would say,
The drinking continued and so did the crime,
I soon got arrested, I'm doing more time.

Remanded for five months, then back up in court,
'I'll get a long sentence', well that's what I thought,
Again I got lucky, again I got free,
'this life as a criminal, aint no life for me'.

But still I kept drinking and then came the crime,
I soon got arrested, I've done it this time,
This crime is so serious, I'm gonna get years,
Have I got a brain between my little ears?

I wish that my brain would stop me from drinking,
Cos drinking means trouble, now when will it sink in?
I've let down my family, I've let down my friends,
If time is a healer, I hope that it mends.

Cos my brain is broken, I can't seem to think,
Cos if it was working, then I wouldn't drink.

Dan Hannam - HMP Dorchester

When will I be free?

When will I be free?

Slave to the system, which I'm conditioned to believe in
Brought up in a dogmatic religion, where I'm born into
Education! Education! Succeed or fail
Have a job and go to work or commit crime and go to jail

I think about my release date, I can't wait to be free
Free to be with my family, so happy and glad
Free to be a man, free to be a Dad
Free to prepare and eat my own food
Free from the prison regime, free from the screws
Free to live life but am I really free
Do I live life or life live me

I get out of prison but I'm still not free
What we call a free society isn't really free to me
I have to get up every day to report to work and I can't be late
I do what my boss tells me to do, this job I really hate
If I rebel then I get the sack
I don't get paid so I can't afford food or the rent for my flat
It's not only me, I have a family to support!
If I don't serve the system, my family is no more

I'm looked at as a failure, no job, no car, no money
Free society is a joke but I'm not finding it funny

So I'm back where I started
When will I be free?

I serve the system; the system doesn't serve me.

Luke Harrison - HMP Risley

My Lying Heart

I'll lie to you babe
You can lie to me
We can lie to each other
Into warm complacency

I can tell you good things
Hide away the bad
Stroke your hair with loving fingers
Stop you feeling sad

You have to lie to me too
Let me know you care
Pretend to open up your heart
And strip your soul down bare

We're only superficial
Our feelings are the same
It'll make no difference when you leave
It made none when you came

Lies are all I have to offer
Lies are all you'll get
Truth will only make us suffer
Leave us emotionally in debt.

Mark Hawkins -
HMP Channings Wood

Rose Tinted Spectacles

We don't tell lies in my house
except to the police
Maybe to the social workers
and busybodies on the street

We don't get beaten by our parents
they don't do drugs or crime
they never turn violent
drunk on their cheap wine

I've never witnessed incest
smelled the fumes of crack cocaine
and if you don't believe me
my siblings will tell you the same!

Mark Hawkins - HMP Gloucester

Together

We've know each other for 16 years
Through good times through bad times
Happy times and sad times

The laughing, the joking
The talking, the shouting
Travelling and sleeping
Eating and drinking
We've done it all together

The pubs, the cinema, the town, the shopping,
Birthdays and Christmas, weekends and Easters
Days out and shows and places we've been
We really have had some great times together

Holidays to France, Spain and Malta
USA, Canada, Italy, Majorca
The list goes on and we've done them all
Side by side together

We are a twosome, a double act, a team
But for a short while I'll continue on my own
Going through the motions the sorrow and pain
I'll put on a front but without any pleasure
Cos you are my soul mate, my partner, my treasure

Like Batman without Robin
Like Laurel without Hardy
Like Chas without Dave

I count the weeks the days and hours
They are known now by numbers not names
Weekends are quiet, lonely and dark
I'm lonely and bored whilst we're apart

So if you thought I would turn, cut you out or leave
Shun or ignore you or turn my back
You were mistaken as I'm still by your side
With my help and support for whatever it's worth

➢

And if you thought that this would be the end
It's not at all, just a new start
It's only a break, a pause or a pit stop
Then we will start all over again.

Step by step you'll start to recover
Things will improve and start to get better
The end of this nightmare is getting closer
The lights getting increasingly brighter

But til then I'll put on my brave face and act
I'll smile for the camera and put on a pose
Though deep down I'm full of emotion
And sometimes I just want to lay there and weep

You're in my mind all of the time
At work and at home both day and night
You're even there during my sleep
And at various times throughout the week

Soon in the future it will be behind us,
A thing of the past, just history
An experience is all it will be
We'll carry on where we left off and
Continue planning the future

So when I get down I just think of the future
When you're back with me
Together, forever!
Just don't leave me again.

Darren Hawkins - HMP Bullingdon

Primal scream

Before I drew my first breath
And cried my first tear,
I popped out my head
To check the coast was clear

Oh no, they've gone and clocked me
And now it's bang on top,
I can feel them trying to pull me free
And there's no way they're going to stop

I ventured into this brand new life
Into a world which was oh so new,
And got a decent slap off the midwife
For looking a lighter shade of blue

Who was she to do that to me?
This is all like a bad dream,
But I thought to myself f*** authority
And let rip with a primal scream.

Warren Heath - HMP Winchester

Heroin

Behold my friends for I am heroin,
Known by all as destroyer of men,.
From where I come nobody knows,
A faraway place where poppies grow.

I come into this country without getting caught,
And now everyday am hunted and sought,
Whole nations have gathered to plan my destruction,
They call me the breeder of crime and corruption.

In cellophane wraps I soon make my way,
To men in their offices and children at play,
From heads of state to lowest of scum,
I give you my word they'll be under my thumb.

I'll make you lie, steal, borrow and beg,
And search for a vein in your arm or your neck,
I'll make you selfish and fill you with greed,
Regardless of colour, religion or creed.

I'll take a rich man and make him poor,
I'll take a virgin and make her a whore,
Make a beautiful women forget her looks,
Make all the students forget their books.

You have heard all my warnings but won't take heed,
Put your foot in the stirrup and mount this great steed,
Hold on fast and hold on real well,
For the great horse of heroin will take you to Hell!!!

Liam Hickson - HMP Lewes

Brave Mask

I try and block out the pain
But I end up feeling shame
Everyday's the bloody same

I'm crying inside
I'm surrounded by people
But I'm alone
My hearts beating
I'm alive
But just existing

All the lads say 'what's up Hodgey'?
I say 'I'm fine I'm just not here'
In truth I'm tearing off my skin
I want to cry but I can't
So I wear my brave mask
Just so the lads won't ask

S Hodgson - HMP Liverpool

Who are these people?

As I sit at my desk quietly at work
both ears wide open, all senses alert,
a thought comes to mind and it troubles me so,
it won't go away, I simply must know.
Who are the people I see before me,
they seem quite content as far as I can see
where are their secrets, where is their pain
is it back in their cells or outside in the rain
They laugh and they joke and I wonder why,
don't they know where they are, are their heads in the sky
Who are these people who hide it so well,
they're not made of wood, this much I can tell.
What is their secret, is it a gift
I wish they would tell me 'cos I need a lift
I'll keep on observing in the hope I might learn
how to cope with this nightmare and achieve what I yearn
Who are these people, God's children them all
and why were they chosen to take the fall
I wish them all well and strength of mind
to see this time through and that peace they may find
So I'm asking you God, look down from your steeple
and answer my question,
Who are these people?

D Hogg - HMP Hull

Hot stuff

You're so sweet
You're so tasty
You're so hot

I love to hold you as I chill
I love to share you with my friends
I love to wake and see you by my bed

Times I hate you, as you're too hot to handle
Yet you soon turn cold
Times I've seen you wetting other's lips
Times you're used for a quick dip

Wanted on each break, I take
Wanted all around the world
Wanted not just by boys, but also girls

People think you're a bit of a drip
People think you're just a square
People know how to make you weak
But with me you're strong

Let me quote these words said of you …
I could kill for you. I would die for you

TEA I LOVE IT!

David Holland - HMP Manchester

Goodbye Girls

I used and abused two ladies each and every day
But they were usin an abusin me in each and every way
Back then I was blind ... really couldn't see
How this brown girl and white lady were really usin me!
Both were just like prostitutes, because they bled me dry
But the levels of pleasure they'd take me to
Would fly me kinda high
If I paid them little there's little they would do
But if I had a roll of notes they'd wallop my mates too
Lady heroin one was called, the other miss cocaine
And if you done them both together
They'd blow your f***in brain
Miss cocaine had a split personality,
She sometimes turned to crack
But either way she'd take you to heaven
While riding on her back
Lady heroin was different,
She'd do you all night long
But many would say that she was dirty
And doing her was wrong
Now and then we'd have a threesome and mix it up a bit
Up and down round and round these girls they were the shit
They got me through some bad times but also in much trouble
They even got me locked in jail quick march and on the double
The police got oh so sick of me they just refused my bail
The judge would say that I'm a fiend and send my arse to jail
Now I've found a decent girl who's love don't cost a pound
And says that she will leave me if them two hoes stick around
Emma's my fiancé's name with a bun in the oven
And I need her in my life right now coz Emma's strong and stubborn
She's there through the bad times and she'll be there through the good
Unlike most me so called mates back in my neighbourhood
Celton's Emma's five year old who thinks the world of me
So a role model to me little soldier I have gotta be
Goodbye I said two months ago to lady heroin and miss cocaine
When I returned back to this place on a sweat-box full of pain
Back then I felt kinda rough when I turned my back on lasses
But two months on I'm bouncin again and doing SDP drug classes!
A course that's giving me tools so I can make better future choices
And I know the judge has my life in his hands, after listenin to big wig voices
My future in his hands, but does he really know what's best for me?
Coz for fifteen years now all they've ever done is lock me up you see
So goodbye girls, the rhymes ok I've said what I needed to say
Now I've to do one day at a time as they tell you to at NA!!

Scott Hornby - HMP Preston

Crack Head

Listen mate, 'coz this ain't funny
Crack cocaine costs more than money,
So if you've never had a pipe
Then let me tell you what it's like.
The first one feels ever so nice
But you never get that feeling twice,
Soon you're out grafting day and night
Just to get your piece of white.
Then you end up in some nick
With a criminal record inches thick,
Then you're brought before the Crown
And the bastard judge says: "Take him down".
But one thing's certain for you and me
Is that we both end up with the same CoD,
So just think on, you'll see I'm right,
He goes by the name of Mr White.

Mark Horrocks - HMP Garth

Realism

The light of liberty dims in our green and
Pleasant land as Orwellian concepts creep
Into society, dismantling democracy.
Under an umbrella of nightmare scenarios
Human rights are removed covertly, adversely
Unnoticed by a populous living in a fallacy of freedom.
A flawed legal system discriminates the
Majority yet protects those policing with impunity;
Immunity from prosecution, even when they kill.
Taxed and restrained by draconian laws,
Conned to engage in predatory wars by politicians
Promising to fulfil the people's will, yet who
Install CCTV to control them.
The role of media spewing government
Propaganda evoke memories of how past dictators
Came to rule and fool the masses; create classes
To implicate.
Our national heroes – Churchill, Nelson and
The like – turn in their graves as people are
Enslaved by muppets; puppets endorsing everything American.
So, descendents of Britannica wake up from
Your trance, reject the dance; enhance right,
Unite, by voting in the next election for
Correction to the status quo.

Dennis Hudson - HMP Manchester

Obama Elect

President Obama; 5th November 2008
First black man as president, through the White House gate
For this day, black people could not wait
Chicago, Illinois his home town appreciates

45 years ago MLK's life was deemed
Martin Luther King expressed his dream
At least his daughter Bernice was there to see
The day black people thought would never be

This day I felt more than ever so proud to be black
When at 4.30am 5/11/08 they said the president was Barack
All the beatings, the lynching and all the attacks
Now the change, our dream … a black man on top

Remember Selma City, Montgomery, they could not vote
And when they campaigned got beaten, hanged by the rope
Civil rights? Black Americans thought there's no hope
Those days when blacks just could not cope

The votes 349 to McCain's 161 could not deprive!
McCain knew his hopes wouldn't stay alive
Palin, the so-called 'lipstick on a pit bull' by his side
They blame her and Bush as the nation decides

In Kenya, his village people jump and sing
Obama! Their brother, son; is now the USA's king
They clap, they dance, they throw, they fling
As they watched Obama, our era's Martin Luther King

He lost his Nan two days before
But how proud she'd have been for sure
If only they had for cancer a cure
She would be here to hear the nation's roar

Now his term in power will surely be a test
And his least mistakes they won't let go to rest
He won it fair, south, east and west
President Obama we wish him the best.

Marcus Humphrey - HMP Risley

Found

If I could find that space between
Of thoughtless peace, before my dreams
That trance-like state of shallow breath
A place of nothing, it's like death.
Would I then tell my dreams to be
As I should like them, joyful glee?
Or should they come, as life, unplanned
Life soft warm breezes, oceans grand?
Yes! This is nature's randomness
And good or bad, the way that's best
'Cos often times my dreams come true,
For there I'm waking next to you.

Paul Hutchinson - HMP Onley

Burn

'Ere bruv, you got a burn mate?
You just got your canteen!
Sort us out
A fouling snout
And I'll do ya one for three'

'Ere bruv, you gotta burn mate?
A skinny one will do.
Give us a smoke
I'm a stand up bloke,
I'd do the same for you!'

'Ere bruv, you gotta burn mate?'
A total stranger asks.
For the past two days
He's looked away
Every time that I've walked past!

'Ere bruv, you got that burn mate?'
I ask my new found friend.
He sucks his teeth,
'don't give me grief!'
I've just been knocked
Again!

C Ingle - HMP Chelmsford

Second Chance

The second chance is better than the first
It feels better, it tastes better
Don't look for it;
You'll recognise it when it comes
The second chance is just around the corner,
Awaiting your acquaintance.

N Jarrett - HMP Swaleside

The Sleeper

A tower stands, not far away
With no walls of brick or stone
Yet trapped within a sleeper lies
Entombed in flesh and bone

This wretched sleeper, for so he seems
Locked away from truth and light
But he does not see his prison walls
Sleeping eyes have no sight

The eternal dream, a life intense
Complete with highs and lows
A constant dream is joy enough
When no waking life I'd known

But the time will come for dreams to end
The sleeper will arise
And see a world bright with life
Through his prison eyes

And fight with sleep's enticing grip
Of dreams that can be fine
Leave joys and sorrows all untrue
For peace and bliss divine

George Jenkinson - HMP Bristol

Despair

Filthy showers, rotten and black
The pad next door stinking of smack
Turn down your music or land on ya back
Carry on son, you'll lose your top rack
The state of the urinals, old, full of mould
Pipes always rattling but the cells are still cold
Got any burn mate, double next week
PO's on his way pal, then I'm back on me feet
I'm off for a boot now, sweet, sweet, sweet.

Why do we do it, the crime and the drugs
Surely we know that we are the mugs
Smack heads and car thieves
Robbers and such
It can't be that all of us don't give a fuck
When will it stop, my life of crime
Right now I reckon, cos this aint for me
I've lost everything now, including my family.

So 12 months left, I'm on the home straight
Keep my head down for 52 weeks
Then I'm back home, back on the streets
But no more drugs and no more crime.
I aint doing this again, a waste of my time
I need to prove the family wrong
Get them back singing, or at least humming my song
I've made my mistakes and I've paid for them dear,
So open the door kids, cos your daddy is near.

Tony Jennings - HMP Leyhill

Bad day

I'm having a bad day, the phone's hung up
Don't talk to me, just shut the fuck up
Any other day I'm a nice chilled bloke
But upset me today and your nose is getting broke
I couldn't tell you why, but I could justify
Ripping someone's head off
So just stay away, I'm having a bad day

Never mind the screws, I'm having a bad day
Piss me off today and I'll kick your fucking head in
I'd bottle up my anger but the bottle is full
Feeling like De Niro, raging like the bull
Trashing my pad, steaming like a train
If you dare to complain
You'll be leaving with a bloodstain
Just stay away, it's not a good day

If you're gonna be around me don't let your mouth slip
Cos I'm well in the mood to give you a fat lip
No human contact and if you interact
Your life is on contract
Your best bet is to stay the fuck away
I'm having a bad day.

Andy Jewitt - HMP Hull

Heart of the country

This land is not mine to sell or trade
I have no claim on these vast acres
Where the crow flies home to roost
A solitary figure
The muddy creek runs deep
But the wattle and daub cottage has long gone
The orchard lies still like a nameless graveyard
In the distance the forest's trees stand to attention
Death whirls in the wind
The whole area now derelict
Devoid of feeling
This was once my home
Yet I feel quite mendicant
For I long since relinquished my hold on this arid desert
I sold out to the highest bidder
Packed my thirty pieces of gold and left
For the bright lights of the big city

But now I have returned to collect the one thing
I left behind
My heart

M Jolley - HMP Birmingham

Detox

This is a good day
Long may it last
Shoes are returned
Plans have been hatched

Tremors receding
Cravings are few
Sweating and nausea
Lessening too

There'll be tears before bedtime
And some in the day
As feelings to run
Fight feelings to stay

But the cavalry's here
It's mounted it's guard
It's stood to attention
The battle'll be hard

I'll call upon angels
To stand at my bed
I'll summon God's spirits
To reclaim my head

I'll plead to God's mercy
For favour and grace
To bless me with wisdom
To return me full face

Matthew Jones - HMP Parc

No View

I look out my window and all I see
Is another building looking back at me
Hear cars passing, people laughing
But the building blocks my view!

Gregory Jones - *HMP Lewes*

The Visit

The room is busy her head is dizzy
Examining faces, she searches for traces
Of recognition
Has he changed – his hair rearranged?
He doesn't wear a beard;
Does he look weird or in poor condition?
He's bald and fat – she recalled that.
'A head like a bowling ball' he'd say,
Eyes that were kind came into her mind
A man that was not very tall
Her face lit up; a man stood up
Her eyes aglow; THAT face I know
Standing out from the crowd.
She wanted to cry
To sob and shout 'why!'
Wanted to scream out loud.
She kept her calm, stepped into arms warm
She huddled and snuggled inside.
The pain was going;
A year on her own
During which she'd nearly died...
... he sat on his own, a man so alone;
He'd waited so long for this,
His throat burned, his stomach churned, but
    still they took the piss
A minute here, a minute there; an extra wait
Stand in line; two at a time, wait by the gate.
He watched her arrive, her face so alive,
Searching amongst the faces
He took a delight, staying out of sight
For that instant recognition.
Her eyes so wide, she hadn't cried
Concealing her own emotion,
Now, by his side, she swelled with pride
Revealing their true devotion.

There were no words their bond was enough,
Two people that should be together
The years had flown and closer they'd grown
Something so right FOREVER.

Tony Joyce - HMP Albany

Ruegan

Kisses in the wind
A clear view goodbye
Turn a corner with a wave of the hand
Never jealous leaving
Bright eyes never leave us
Down the glen, forest of fruit
Fresh spring wells
Foxes plenty
No farmer with gun
Blackbird sings, on a hazel tree
Night falls, bright eyes
Never fade
Back in the room
Sun don't shine
Bees don't sting
Little blue

Declan Kavanagh -
HMP High Down

Cleaner's Lament

In prison while flicking my mop
An epiphany forced me to stop
My soul won't be saved
The road to justice won't be paved
And to public concern, I'm no more than a sop!

Daniel Kessler - HMP Lindholme

I only want to talk

Sleeping on the streets
Invisible to caring
People walk on by
Not giving or sharing
They all thought it was drink
Or drugs that I needed
If only they'd stopped and
Listened to my pleading
Silently inside I was asking
For their prayers
To make my life worthwhile
Better, like theirs
Why didn't they stop and talk to me
But they were just blinkered
Unable to see
Now I am here
In prison today
Still nobody stops
I still have no say

Stephen Kidd - HMP Preston

The Easy Life

Don't think it through, just do the job
Does it really matter who you rob?
If you think you can spare the time
Then go ahead and do the crime

Who gives a fuck, they're only mugs
Just go and sell more class A drugs
He won't notice, the blokes really thick
He'll never know just what you nick

They won't catch us mate 'cos we're the pros
We're just way too fast when on our toes
Insurance scams or an armed robbery
These are the jobs for you and me

Some easy money, let's go raise more cash
We'll be in and out mate, in a flash
No 9-5 jobs, those roles are a joke
Go find some wimp and give him a poke

Why hesitate now eh? You know what to do
It's an easy lift mate, you know the coo
But you will get caught I think you'll find
And there's many in here who had your like mind

Andrew King - HMP Coldingley

Prison Bullshit Blues

Slam the goddamn door to kill the lights
Prelude to eternal sleepless nights

Keys jangle, tempting your senses with freedom
Freedom
Lost in a tide of voices
Why the hell am I here?

Shithouse blues
Made all the wrong moves

Razor wire vision cuts into the accepting skyline
The clouds don't judge me on my crime
These bullshit prison blues help me pass the time

Find me a guitar with barbed wire strings
Wire a harmonica to my silent mouth
Play those f***in' blues till I bleed my crime
From the core of my soul

Socialise daily with unfamiliar faces
I am distanced by design
Now I'm forced to tow the line
Listen as they confess to petty pointless crimes

Who am I to judge?

Prison bullshit blues
The same old tunes.

Philip Kirk - HMP Ranby

Back in the day

Back in the day there was no telly
Piss pots ruled and the cells were smelly
Bang up a plenty with nothing to do
You hated the screws and they hated you
Escape was the gym, or a tug in the sack
Now it's a pill or a lung full of smack

Back in the day, there was no phone
Food was scarce we were all skin and bone
Beatings a plenty, our screams unheard
All part and parcel of doing your bird

Back in the day we had no voice
We put up with the shit coz we had no choice
We danced with the rats and lived with the fleas
Now it's big systems and DVDs
Curtains and bedspreads, kettles as well
Your very own toilet, no longer the smell
Protein and keratin, tuna for a sarnie
By the time you get out you can look like Arnie!

Steve Lewtas - HMP Dovegate

Wind scream

I heard a blackbird's voice
snapped off by a sudden
savage gust, and this
elemental fury
would batter dust mote
towering mountain.

Rising to a sonic whistle
it would own the night-
rattle and worry the window
as if there's no place
no space or refuge
where it could not go.

Like a thunderclap within the cranium
illuminating a glum, grizzled
perspective on pathos,
I'd no wish for any season
so primitive, emotive
reverberant with loss!

In little bursts of blind rage
leaving carnage in town and field,
whistling, howling, screaming
out some natural protest,
throwing hammer blows
at everything living.

Bricked up in my brooding corner
I imagine, the judge is out again -
banging the gavel
banging a nail into a coffin
banging home consequence,
all the pain as well.

Rain now with the wind
splashing, spattering upon the pane -
furious cascade within a dream
within a moment while living in a reverberating can,
listening to the wind scream!

Paul Lumsden - HMP Dumfries

Bumblebee

If I was a flower
And the sun shone on me
Perhaps I'd play host
To the odd bumblebee
Wings that could fly me
To the here
And the there
I'd live for a day
Without much of a care

I tell you
One is too many
And a thousand is not enough
The life that I've lived
The smooth and the rough
The reasons were none
The excuses were many
I made them all
Until I'm not left with any

I look into the mirror
I'm not sure who I see
In my place this old man
Where a young man used to be
I go back to my cell
My own private little hell
I think about the flowers
And the odd bumblebee
Wings that might fly me
And defy gravity

Del MacDonald -
HMP Wealstun

Speak to a Listener

Here I am, all alone in prison
It stinks in here coz there's no one to listen
I hate it when the door locks,
Coz all I have is my digi-box
Hey look, it's almost time for dinner
I can't eat that muck, I'd be classed as a sinner
Ma cell mate bolts it right past me
He's running so fast, like he needs a pee
Ya got all your hommies doin their talk
Why is it they are so slow when they walk?
Dinner's over, it's now time to sleep
I wake up not knowing the day of the week.
Ma pad mate is taking a huge dump
Oh my God bruv, he's got me in a rite hump
Door opens, and it's time for education
Whoa God, a bit of civilisation
I'm sitting at ma desk wishing I was at home
When it suddenly dawns on me I'm still alone
Education is over, it's time for some food
Why is it the serving guys are so rude?
Association comes and time to make a call
My girl answers and says my son's had a fall
I should be out there caring for him
But I'm inside, wishing I wasn't such a din
Time for bang up now, God I hate it!
Ma pad mate is listening to Abba! Tit!
Jumpin on my bed, it's time to count sheep
Can't sleep now, all I do is weep
Here I am, all alone in prison
It stinks in here, there's no one to listen
If you are feeling alone
Reach for the phone, speak to a Listener
Speak to them, they help
They really do
They may help you

Joseph MacLeod - HMP Albany

Safe to cry

The sun don't shine like it used to do
And the rain just keeps on pouring down on me
It makes me feel like
I'm in my prison cell.
Blinding light shining down on me
I hear the footsteps of the watchman as he passes by
Then I know now, it's safe to cry.
I've been searching for the meaning of my life
Look for answers but stay awake all night
That's when I need you to hold me tight.
I close my eyes and I can see for a million miles
And there before me is your warm and loving smile
Those were the days my love, those were the days.
You took away all my fear and loneliness
Now we are together is it God that I should bless
Or should I thank my lucky stars.

Gordon Maddocks - HMP Blakenhurst

Interim

Looking out from the inside
Where past meets present.
White noise penetrates the soul
Deep scares need clarity.
Holding onto today
For the touch of tomorrow.
The bland taste of life
As days collapse into flavours.
Sweet smells of the past
Rekindle the future.

Carl Mallinson - HMP Bristol

Who's that girl?

Here I am lost in time
Trying to find myself
Can't see clearly
My vision is too cloudy

Stripped of my identity
I look in the mirror
But I don't know this face

No shampoo to wash my hair
No gel to style it
My hair is all messy
I have no makeup
My face is bare

Who is this person I see right now
I've been taken apart
Piece by piece then glued back
Together again.

When I look into the mirror
It's not me that I see
Just some strange girl
That keeps looking at me.

Lorraine Manzi - HMP Bronzefield

Political Chameleon

All politicians sound the same
Tories and Labour playing the game
Taxing the poor so they can stay rich
I think it's time with our votes we should switch
Should we try Liberal or lets all go Green
Use our brains, do yer know what I mean?
Tressal had vision and said what he saw
Men in power rinsing the poor
Join a union and use your vote
Get off your arse and put on your coat
Remember Thatcher and all of her lies
New Labour's the same open your eyes
The babble they speak doesn't make sense
There's no excuse to sit on the fence
This is how the poor were robbed.
She sold off BA she sold off BP
She sold a lot more for a measly fee
If I robbed yer telly and hi-fi too I'd go to jail on a 6 to 2
If I sold yer them back would yer know the score?
Maggie done the same and ripped off the poor
She took on the miner and forced him to give in
Ask yer self this, how did she win?
With state TV and the arm of the law
Their spirits were broken and now they are poor
The nurses were next, our caring profession
Up in arms but for wages protection
Then came the teachers and dockers as well
When Maggie dies will she go to hell?
Back to today and nothing has changed
Spend billions on wars and no one to blame
The children still suffer and we all worship oil
Don't care for the planet and poison the soil
The rich still cut corners chasing the wealth
It's the poor that pays and it shows with their health

Edward Marriette - HMP Liverpool

Ode to a dead towel!

Farewell my friend, I loved you well
But now I have to say you smell
You've stood by me through thick and thin
But now you're ready for the bin.

I've tried to treat you with great care
But you clearly are the worse for wear
On countless morns you left me dry
You sad departure makes me cry.

You covered me when I was bare
And I walked around without a care
But now you're old and are so tattered
That my ego is at times quite shattered.

For your fabric I had much to pay
Now through it I see light of day
You dried my floor when I washed my cell
All in all you've done quite well.

I worked on you with needle and cotton
Although your fabric was quite rotten
I fixed you up, you looked ok
But you lasted one more day.

I'll think of you with great pleasure
Now you're going to your leisure
I wish you well in your new roll
Blocking up that draughty hole!

Stephen Marron - HMP Gartree

Memoirs of an illegal immigrant

They don't know me but they think they do,
Smile at me like everything cool
They say I'm illegal so I can't go to school
What else to do except join the crew?

Left my country in search of a better life
But I'm not allowed to work, not expected to do crime
Like Tanya said 'it's like beating a child
Then telling them not to cry'

I blagged it to get a job instead of doing crime
And for that now I'm doing time
My main goal is just to survive
I do what I do coz I aint doing fine
Barefoot ghetto boy, keep my eyes on the prize!

They know what it is in Zimbabwe
But the immigration still tryin to ship me back
Just so they can send me 'Food Aid'
Don't feed me, I would rather work!

Was raised in the jungle, that made me a soldier
Spent half my life looking over my shoulder
One luv to my brothers in the same struggle
Tomorrow aint promised that's why we hustle!

Johnson Mashoko - HMP Lewes

Reach For The Sky

Staring at the world through the bars
I see a tree, cold bricks, exercise yard,
Frightened and scared of what's in store
They scream and shout and slam the door.
Shaking and numb, full of despair
I look through the window, there's nothing there,
As I look out all I can see
Is just me, the bars, and a tree.
The months roll by and into years
My view has changed I've lost the fears,
Now through the bars there is a tree
Standing tall …looking back at me.
Waving its branches, without a sound
So strong and tall, firm to the ground,
Caressing the sky with your gentle sway
A perch for a bird, who has lost his way;
Dancing for the sun and bowing to the stars
Saluting Jupiter, Venus and Mars.
Autumn comes you've changed your attire
Orange and gold, burning like fire,
Winter arrives and strips you bare
Looking so naked with nothing to wear.
Jack to the rescue with sequins so neat
Snowdrops and crocus adorn your feet
Glittering and shimmering as the robins sing
Looking majestic, waiting for spring.
Natural beauty in all your glory
I've learnt a lot from your story
Without the drink, my eyes are clear
I've dealt with the root of all my fear;
Summer comes you're dressed all in green
Full of blossom, just like a queen,
Blowing kisses to all, as they pass by
A carpet of petals, tells me why
We can all stand tall and reach for the sky.

Angie Mason - HMP Morton Hall

Understanding my cell mate

One minute life can feel so sweet
Till that day comes when you're blown off your feet
Taken away from everything and out of society
You soon realise you're no longer a priority

When the sun rises and we get out of bed
We get mentally prepared for the day ahead
Looking out the window at the fields in the distance
Then there's the bars causing this resistance

There's no point having a moan
Like it or not, this is our new home
No matter how loud we roar
No one can hear, once we're behind this metal door

No one can understand our pain
Sat in this concrete box, with only our thoughts on our brain
But I've met a new friend, he's a lot like me
Every time I look in the mirror, he's all I can see

Me and him get on really well
We have to, we share a cell
99% of the time he's such a nice bloke
We sit here together and have a laugh and a joke

Then there's the 1% when he flips his lid
I can see it in his eyes, he's just a scared kid
BANG, he's gone, turned into that nasty geezer
I look at him and say, mate I don't wanna be anywhere near ya

I stare him in the eye
He stares straight back and starts to cry
I feel his pain, I know what he's going through
I give him a hug, tell him I'm here for you

I've been there for him when he's feeling down
He's helped me get my feet back on the ground
Even though he's entertaining and amusing
It sometimes feels a little confusing

Hold on a minute, I know this guy
Oh yer, it's me, myself and I
I now know without a doubt
I know myself inside out

23 hours a day in the company of yourself
Makes me wonder if it's good for your health

Steve McCarthy - HMP Lewes

In Memoriam – 9/11

It is hard to believe what happened that day,
Thousands of people just blown away
Hard to believe before eight forty five,
They were walking, talking, breathing, alive.

It is hard to believe that Allah could smile;
Bless and condone an act so vile.
Hard to believe when they hi-jacked the planes,
Those sons of Jihad were human – had names.

It is hard to believe what man did to man,
Vainglorious and cruel to further a plan.
Hard to believe we've learned nothing at all,
From that sad, sad day, when the towers did fall.

It is hard to believe the lives now lost,
In Baghdad and Helmand – a terrible cost.
Hard to believe what happens each day,
My fellow beings just blown away

Gerard McGrath - HMP Dovegate

The Test

I arrived on Friday night
Scared about my future plight
I must get through this test I know
I'll just keep quiet, go with the flow

I settle down in my new home
Trying to avoid the mental moan
The wind is whistling fast outside
Seagulls hitch an easy ride

When I awake I feel real cold
I'd say something but I'm not bold
Breakfast time has come already
I must admit I sure am ready

I'm worried now about this jail
It is a test I must not fail
I'll do the tasks that I am set
My freedom is a long way yet

J McHale - HMP Acklington

Behind these Bronzefield Walls

Behind these Bronzefield walls
The fields aint bronze
Nor is the colour of my black skin
There is no colour here, within these metal gates
No African light, no African sky, no African sun,
To glow my face.
No class or racial discrimination,
Because there resides no race here.
No Japanese or Chinese
No British or Asian
No Jamaican or Romanian
No Ethiopian or Somalian
No Nigerian or Congolese
No Irish or Scottish.

All women here move with the same pace,
At the same time.
Breakfast time, education or work time.
Lock-down time,
You see these women here all on the same page,
Same chapter in a book entitled HMP Bronzefield
They move within the same space that has robbed
Them of all grace.
A space that holds pain firmly within its grasp
A space that forces smiles and laughter
Awaiting reality to steal it all away
With the cruel break of dawn.
A space that slices deep within my veins,
Leaving my memories of yesterday
Drowning in a sea of blood.

Behind these Bronzefield walls,
Our faces have no names,
Instead numbers are attached to identify our movements.
So limited are those movements,
Monitored calls, monitored letters.
The price we pay for desperate circumstances
Only dreams are free, here on the inside.
Because it is my dreams that allow me to travel
While my feminine body lies behind these bars.
Still in my dreams I am free,
Free to travel back home to Africa
And embrace my loved ones.
I travel back home searching for the me I left behind.

Reassuring myself that I shall soon return,
Return to the land of my forefathers.

Behind these Bronzefield walls.
We are mothers separated from our young ones
We are lovers longing for familiar faces
We are wives estranged from our husbands
We are grandmothers longing for our grandchildren's
Playful chatter.
We are women dressed in pants,
Forced to denounce our images of sexuality.

Behind these Bronzefield walls.
We are artists, artistically recreating and remoulding
Our broken lives
We are writers, storytellers, narrating our past
We are teachers, teaching each other
How to get through the days.
We are chaplains, giving spiritual hope to those
Who seek it.
We are chefs, feeding a nation of female prisoners
We are assistants, assisting our fellow sisters
How to cope within the prison system.

Behind these Bronzefield Walls.
I do not look forward to morning,
So cold and uninviting.
As I look out through my barred window
I wonder if the flowers here are prisoners too.
Will they ever know the difference of this life
And the one beyond?
I turn away from the cloudy skies
I want no reminder of an ongoing life
Though I am counting down the days towards my release
I still wish that I could make time stand still
On my behalf,
Await me to retrace my steps back,
Back to my last day of freedom,
My last free breath,
My last free thought, my last free words uttered.
I want to go back to my last free dance on the outside
Because behind these Bronzefield walls
The fields will never be bronze like Africa
These fields will never be free like Africa.

Naledi Moet-Lottering - HMP Bronzefield

A vision of hell

My weeping eyes opened unto a world of pain
And any other kind of life seemed a world away
Within the vision I peeped, my father was wax
A living figurine that was melting as my world collapsed

I tried to scream but no sound arose
Is this a dream I wondered but then my wondering closed.
For then my mind went blank, as my eyes took to the next sight
What I did see next was the epitome of fright

My mother, blood of my blood and a caring kind soul
Was nothing more than ashes that lay scattered, blacker than coal
And how did I know these horrifying remains were that of my whole earth?
Through word of the beast who spoke in tongues, as he revealed his blood thirst

My surroundings were hellish to the very most extreme
Body upon body, a fleshy wall of human being
Upon each face, there lay a tortured expression
True terror formed these walls, of that there's no question

The walls moaned as I stood in the shadow of death
Ready for my dance with the devil, it was his final request
Then there he appeared, and he was a vision of putrid innards
He was my childhood closet monster and my fear of school dinners

He moved closer toward me and I started to run
But I stayed on the spot like a cartoon, or like a nightmare had begun

He came upon me and entwined with my flesh
Until I was inside his insides, hearing the sounds of digest

Then all was black, and I ceased to exist
Until my weeping eyes opened and I was back at the start of all this

Kieran Mooney - HMP Forest Bank

Paranoid Prisoner

Are the walls closing in on me?
Is my life going to change drastically?
Will I lose the ones I hold to my heart?
Will they get used to us being apart?
Will my wife decide I am no more?
Independent now, I'm so unsure.
Will they all still miss me in three years or so?
Not needed now, will I have to go?
This is how prison makes you feel,
Like you no longer have any more appeal.
Each day you think they'll need you less,
You go to bed, your head in a mess.
Yes they'll manage they won't need me,
Just a matter of time and they will see
They never needed me all along,
I need reassurance, please tell me I'm wrong.
One day I'll be walking out the gate
And my family and me will celebrate,
But if on release … no children … no wife
Then I've lost everything, no point to life.

David Morris - HMP Featherstone

One Day

It's the root of much evil that poisons my people
As dangerous as any weapon and ten times as lethal
My window to what's happening outside the gate
Reveals it's a brave new world AKA a police state
Tougher sentences, conviction on suspicion
Let's knock down that hospital and build another prison
Newborns fingerprinted, DNA taken at birth
Still got the hardest cavemen running the earth
Traded their clubs for a Glock 9, flogging for jail time
Flying a flag now classed as a hate crime
Laws against dreaming, get taxed just for breathing
Hear the sound of the beast, get shot down by the demon
When did this war on terror become a war on freedom?
Laws broken, bent and twisted to encompass anyone breathing
Privacy invaded, grand database, face recognition
CCTV up the arse when I'm shitting and pissing
Enough is enough it's time to make a stand
Since the guns were outlawed we must fight hand to hand
Send the word to the foot soldiers, round 'em up
This here's our world which we built from the ground on up
A massive uprising let's take back the streets
We outnumber the army, politicians and police
The government's budgets blown on war, never on peace
Guns turned on their own people, missiles released
They pushing the button and the end is nigh
They forced our hand now we're all gonna die
Everything vaporised as the end of man approaches
How ironic, the worlds still run by cockroaches

Mr C - HMP Wealstun

Smile

One true love for one real lover
I talk of a girl who's my baby's mother
With a heart so pure a love so great
I can only explain her as my soul mate
A special women she'd make a perfect wife
But the path I took led to a different life

My criminal ways went from bad to worse
For the last 10 years it's been a curse
Acting bad riding it tough
If truth be known I've had enough
On this path, around I should turn
But can I change, will I learn?

I've tried many faiths looking for a sign
I so need this to be my final time
How many times do I have to fall
So many times over this wall
Many of the 80,000 are in this boat
Riding the system staying afloat

So as I prepare for another try
A life in prison for what and why
It will be hard but I have what it takes
As this cycle hardly breaks
I shall do it and do it in style
Upon release I'll wear my biggest smile

Stephen Murphy - HMP Bristol

The Parole Hearing

Question
So tell me Murty, how was your life as a youngster?
Answer
'Ruthless' was my style as a juvenile
Ran with a gang
Sold smack in the meanwhile
'Bankin' specialized in skankin
Whites, Mexicans, Brothers and others.
'Daily' it's all about comin up
Makin sure no punk YOs are runnin up
To girls I'm a bad boy havin fun
Lock back ready as I'm walkin through Glasgow
'Terrible' never listened to my mother
Went in one ear, out the other
Ran my gang well undercover
I'll call a girl by her name
But I aint no lover
I'm in it for the cash
Bitches get screwed, then used for the stash
'Rollin' an runnin from the police
Brother don't you know, you can't judge a thief
I'm pure convict, love being criminal
Leave your car open, skanked for your stereo
Hard-n-raw, no regard for the law

Question
Were you ever caught slippin?
Answer
'Hell naw' just love puffin ma blaw
An gettin real drunk don't mean shit to me
My Daddy told me, that's the way shits meant to be
An if anybody's gettin on ma nerves
They'll get beat, skanked, rolled, shanked,
So you know who I am
An if you don't like it, I really don't give a damn

Question
Could you explain what it means when you so call skank somebody?
Answer
'Waitin' for some people to leave
I got another trick up ma sleeve
Step by step to the back of the house
Lock in, all the lights are out.
Grab the door, an it's locked, so
Easily make my way to the window
Lift it up slow, cause it takes timin
Look around, then I climb in
Once inside, I start takin

Cause you know, there's no time for shakin
Get what you're gonna get, front an centre
Or get 5 years for breakin and enter
Move quickly, but no runnin
Ssssshhhhh, I hear somebody comin
Hear the front door key, so I flee
Out the back, with a fist full a jewellery
Over the wall, don't fall.
Wipe ma sweat, cause that was a close call
getting skanked by me is a lesson
So, is there any more questions?

Question
Yes, as a matter of fact there is, have you ever been involved in like a robbery or a hold up?
Answer
'Yep' There's the store
But don't point,
Walk inside and case the joint
One man behind the counter, another in the back
Go out to the car an load the gat
Grab the ski mask, here's the task
Go in broke, come out with cash.

Question
Were you slick?
Answer
'Yeah' you gotta be cunnin
Told the co-accused, to leave the car runnin
Walked in, said 'this is a robbery'
Give me the money, it's just ma hobby
Fill the bag old man, don't lag
I want money, beer and a pack a zig zags
The man in the back had a camera
So he came out to test my stamina
Against the YRB, so he took one
Fell to the floor, so I run
Back to the stoler, said 'punch it'
Took the gun then dumped it
I'm not like Robin Hood, cause I want more
Steal from the rich, hang with the poor
My pockets need fattening, you see
It don't matter to me
Feel like nobody is badder than me

Question
Is all that true?
Answer
I don't lie, you see, I'm not Mr Nice Guy

PAROLE REJECTED!

Alexander Murty - Bar Baydos, Costa Cell Sol (AKA HMP Barlinnie)

Tottenham

The north of the Thames
On a council estate
Train stations here and train stations there
Trident police trying to stop the guns
Eastern European immigrants, Irish and Blacks
Never any peace in this
Haringey borough
Armed gangs fighting, robbing and selling drugs this is
My manor

Ricky Mutton - HMP Wayland

Me ... You

Me: Why do you fall silent? There's been no word for days
You: I feel like I'm drowning
Me: Why do you make me cry? Do you like this? DO YOU??
You: I stared too long at the sun and now I'm blind, I can't see you ...
Me: Why do you treat me like a toy? Do you enjoy this?
You: Be patient. Don't be like me (...I'm slowly coming back to life, only then can we play)
Me: How long will I live?
You: Eternal life, that's how long.
Me: Do you want to be eternal too?
You: No thanks, not today.

Charlie Nokes - HMP Downview

Love and Sorrow

I know you'll never love me
And this is why I cry
I'll never feel your hand in mine
Or hear you softly sigh
I know you'll never miss me
Or notice that I've gone
To me you are somebody
To you I am no-one
I know you'll never cry for me
I'll never cross your mind
You'll never waste a thought on me
I'll always find the time
I know you'll never look for me
The way I look for you
Each face you see is different
Each woman I see is you
I know you'll never lose your heart
The way that I lost mine
They say that time's a healer
To me there is no time
I know you'll never love me
And this is why I cry
Although my body's living
My heart is bound to die
I know you'll never love me
And this is why I cry

Marcus O'Neill - HMP Reading

Oh greedy cockroach!

Oh greedy cockroach
Not in my cell
You cause me grief
You give me hell
I'm paying my penance
I'm doing my time
Come and scavenge another time
Come near me I'll seal your fate
Size ten Reeboks, sorry mate
Too late
You lay there squashed now
Just sticky goo
You should have stayed away
Like I told you to
Oh greedy cockroach is no more
He's now a part of my cell floor.
RIP Cocky the Roach

Oz - HMP Maidstone

Dedicated to Cocky the Roach,
gone but never forgotten

Gay and proud

'Batty man', 'poof', 'faggot', you name it … I've been called it,
The teasing and torment for six months I stalled it
At the start I pretended I was straight
With a nice blonde girl whose physique was great,
But one day like a knob I let it slide
I said I had a boyfriend on the outside.
It was a mistake yea, but to tell you the truth
It was worth the punches, kicks and snapped tooth,
Because now I can say, scream out loud …
I am gay, happy … and proud.

Paul Palmer - HMP Edmunds Hill

The Thief

Golden Virginia
Not Amber leaf
Rich pickings for
A notorious thief
Won't let up
Won't get a job
Won't pay his own way
At the prison shop

Some stuff is missing
From people's cells
Back from work they're on
Their bells
The officer comes
And walks away
Said, leave your door open
And that's the price you pay

Lying in their cell
Smoking other people's burn
I think they're the ones that
Will never learn

Tony Palmer -
HMP/YOI Norwich

Life's Deal

Some cons say life's over
I feel mine's just begun
I turned up for court,
Didn't want to be on the run.
I was killing myself
Slowly from the inside
I was a 'Jack the Lad' dealer
But it was misguided pride.
Snorting all the profits
Barely staying out of debt
Now all of those actions
I sorely regret.
But I know that being banged up
Has prolonged my life
I just wish I'd learned earlier
Could have saved all this strife.
My wife and my daughters
Whilst not filled with glee
Realise now I'm drug free
They'll see much longer of me.
So even though they'll miss me
For two and a half years
I should live much longer
And prolong my death's tears

Ian Parkinson - HMP Haverigg

Jack The Lad

Most of them know him
As Jack the Lad
A loving husband
The perfect dad
Because what they can't see
Is behind a door,
A wife and two kids
Shook to the core
He spends every penny
On women and booze,
A wife sat at home
Kids without shoes
Holding each other
They hear him come in,
A deafening silence
The drop of a pin
Pissed up again
He gives no warning,
Without provocation
Fists are swarming
With gritted teeth
Blows reign down,
The end result
Of a night on the town
A relentless attack
Bruised and battered,
He swings with a right
A cheekbone is shattered
Now shaking with fear
Children cry out,
Hoping and praying
Someone can help
People can hear
But won't intervene,
Ignorance is bliss
Whilst children scream
With broken ribs
And a torn up dress,
She's heaped on the floor
In a bloody mess
Because hidden from others
Jack is a cheater,
A shameless, spineless
Gutless wife beater.

Liam Phipps - HMP Onley

Dreamer

I'm dreaming of you, each and every night,
You're getting closer, you're nearly in sight.
Just as I touch you I hear the door,
My eyes are open, you're there no more.

At first it hurts, the pain immense,
Sweating like mad, all my muscles are tense.
I take deep breaths and start to chill,
You'll be back tonight, I know you will.

Everywhere I go I'm in my bubble,
Keeping quiet and out of trouble.
Thinking of what we'll do this time,
We go together like lemon and lime.

Tonight comes and I struggle to sleep,
I can't wait to see my little Bo-Peep.
Suddenly you're there and looking really fine,
I'm so happy and everything's going divine.

Unfortunately this dream can't last forever,
Sooner or later we'll be back together.
Our nightmare though will soon be over,
I'll be back home with you 'My Lover' XXX

Kevin Poole - HMP Holme House

For my wife Katie, doing a great job at home with the kids and everything else.

Jean Sprackland came today!

Jean Sprackland came today!
- but I was late, and so damn annoyed!
- 'cos of stoopid 'meds'
And 'cos I was late, I could only peep
- round some HUGE guy
- who kept movin' all the time !?*!?
she wouldn't have noticed me, as I
sat, snatching photos of her
whenever she came into view.
And it was her words
That were the revelation.
She spoke so eloquently, cutting
To the quick of a thing

And reading poetry that has magic inside it.
I was mesmerized by her hands…
When she talked
She has beautiful L..o..n..g fingers
- that flex and grasp the air
As she speaks.

Like two baby Octopi
On the end of her arms
That are itchy
With interesting rings.
She said we should look
For things that we think are not significant
- but actually are?
I sat mesmerized and I thought
Despite her **Octopi** issues
I Love Jean Sprackland!
And in amongst me fallin' in love
Kieran Phillips stole my pen

Tony Pope - HMP Garth

Jean Sprackland is a renowned British author. My creative writing group were fortunate enough to be visited by her..

Shadow on my bars

The shadow on my bars stretches across my wall
Wide enough for me to crawl
Crawl through the bars and to my home
Where my once true love now lies alone
I wish I could be standing there
Brushing my fingers through her lovely red blonde hair
But now our love has come to this horrible end
Goodbye my true lover
Goodbye my true friend.

David Prior - HMP Peterborough

The Poem's Trap

I'm writing on this board
within these four walls.
Asian five foot ten tall
can anyone hear me?
I'm giving you a call
Can anyone see me?
I'm behind this steel door
I've been here
I don't know how long for.
I'm gonna stay here
don't know how long any more.
If you open this metal flap
you will see me: perhaps
you could pass me a map
so I can escape this poem's trap

Abz Rauf - HMP Grendon

The Police Visit

Two policemen came to see me
Pretending to be nice
They brought me chocolate biscuits
And a gin and lemon with ice
They said my hair looked tidy
And my shoes were nice and clean
And if I told them what I had done
They would get me some ice cream
I said can I have a raspberry one
If I told them about a bank
They really got excited
One even had a w***
They both got out their notepads
And pen out on their knees
Because I had informed them
I would take some TICs
They both got busy writing
About the bank job and who was on it
I would sell my f***ing brother
For a double gin and tonic

Clovis Razak - HMP Full Sutton

Mr Naughty

So little miss you grew tired of grass,
MDNA, cocaine and hash
Then someone you thought to be a true friend
Said 'Let me introduce you to Mr Heroin'.
Well little miss before you start fooling with me
Let me tell you how it's gonna be,
First I'll seduce you and make you my friend
Then you'll be mine right till the end.
You'll deceive your friends
You'll cheat and lie
All because you want to get high
Con some money
Even sell your soul
Is there anything else to fill this black hole?
Others will preach
But you won't be told
It's time you realised I'm more expensive than gold!
You'll try to escape but you cannot hide
It's only me that can warm your insides
The hot flush the cold sweats
Your itchy veins
How you crave for my little brown grains
I'll leave you for dead
If you run away
Knowing you'll return
My debt you must pay
One day you'll turn and in the mirror look
Where is the girl who's looks I have took
Haggard and drawn
Sucked from within
Oh my darling you've become so thin
So little miss
Remember this ode
Before you decide
To take my road
When life looks grim
And the world so dark
There's no turning back
Until death then we'll part.

Annabelle Rogers & Jackie Sheppard -
HMP Send

The Light In The Tunnel

'Take him down!' My world implodes
My deepest fears to all exposed
Darkness, sorrow, regret, despair
Anger, hatred, without a care
'Keep your head down, you'll soon be out'
Inside I scream 'LET ME OUT!'

The time has come to see it through
Accept the punishment that I am due
Cat C, Cat D, early release?
Hopes in the darkness there to tease
Time to move on, take the blame
My family outside must bear the shame

Calm and composed, I see the light
Gone is the anger, the swiftness of fight
The tunnel surrounds me, the end draws near
My family are waiting, their laughter I hear
Reborn and enlightened, their love awaits
Until they hold me again outside of these gates

Simon Rowe - HMP Everthorpe

Why Am I Here?

Why am I here? What have I done?
I've done nothing wrong, I've hurt no-one
It was not me, I was not there
Does anyone listen? Does anyone care?

A wing, B wing, C wing, D
Officers, screws wherever I be
Gates, bars, keys and locks
Rules, regulations and prison socks

Protection of self? Community good?
Confinement, entrapment, it boils my blood
Treatment, employment, probation, resentment,
Sadists, masochists in their element

Acceptance, enlightenment, religion, belief
No thanks to the system or my useless brief
I'll soon be out, free at last
Whatever I've done just left in the past

Why was I here? What had I done?
I had done nothing wrong I had hurt no-one
It was not me, I was not there
Did anyone listen? Do I really care?

Simon Rowe - HMP Everthorpe

It's just another day ...

Not a lot to do but to sit and stew
And think about yer sen

All day long, preaching right and wrong
Banged up with other men

Hardly a day, when you don't say
'try not to feel so sad'

Trying to cope, hanging onto hope
Before you go bloody mad

Staring into space, despair on your face
Depression coming back

Mind in a spin, what a state you're in
As you hit the snack

It's just another day ...

Mike Ruane - HMP Armley

A mother's tale

We look through the same sky
But you cannot see me
We breathe the same air
But you cannot feel me
We feel the same cold
But I cannot keep you warm

We speak the same language
But we cannot communicate
We love each other
But we cannot demonstrate
I am a mother
You are a son
And nothing can ever stop that

Claudia Santos -
HMP New Hall

HMP

These walls have heard much silent pain
On every brick is scribed a name
The mortar lines are faint to see
Artexed with mankind's misery.
An en-suite in the corner stands
To wash the system from my hands
A plastic fork, mug and spoon
Locked inside a timeless room
Do your graft, score some gear
Shoulders back; show no fear
Door bangs open, time to give
Your worst nightmare with a shiv
Trade your goods from off a line
Easy blokes, just doin time
Paint a teardrop on your face
Miles behind the human race
Cold steel door, sleepless nights
Caught hands down, bang to rights
Thinking of a place called home
Blank it out, heart of stone
Lost in time, too blind to see
Time soon served at HMP

Paul Sarvent - HMP Everthorpe

Lifer's life

Wake up in the morning
Start yawning and stretching
My breakfast needs fetching
Keys jangling
Doors banging
Gone are the days of hanging
Make a cuppa tea
Go to the servery
Then kick back
In my pad
Waiting for the call
Some screw bawls
'Labour and classes'
No gate passes
An exodus of the masses
To the classes and the shops
Tick tock
The clock never stops
Sweatshop, cheap employment
No enjoyment
Silly pay
Mind decay
Never mind
The daily grind moves on.

This is the life of lifers
Life in a day
Day in a life
This is the lifer's life.

One hours exercise
No hellos or goodbyes
Dry your eyes
Stop the cries
And the sighs
If you fall you can rise
Lunch time lock up
Stock up
Get some fuel
Energy for the afternoon duel
This journey can be cruel

➤

Stay cool
Don't lose it
Choose it
Freedom is the prize
Blue skies
Cool breeze
Come and go as you please.

This is the life of lifers
Life in a day
Day in a life
This is the lifer's life

Day dreamers
Dreams are for believers
This is a lifer's jail
No leavers
Just re-cats
C Cats and step backs
Maybe a sideways move
You wouldn't wanna be in my shoes
No date for release
The pressure doesn't cease
Offending behaviour courses
Lack of resources
Less marriage
More divorces
Bad choices
Hearing voices
Voices scream
As I dream
My dream of freedom
Will come
One day..

This is the life of lifers
Life in a day
Day in a life
This is the lifer's life

Andy Senior - HMP Gartree

That Thing

I'm sick of that thing staring at me
From the corner of the room
It costs me a pound a week
And all it brings is doom and gloom
I've unplugged it from the wall
And unplugged from my soul
Because as long as it's in my life
It will always be in control
If you don't know what I'm saying
Or understand what I mean
Some of you call it telly
And some call it TV
If you like life with honesty
And live to seek the truth
Don't watch that thing called Telly
It don't back the facts with proof
TV is just a fairytale
Of how it says that life should be
By getting rid of your telly
Is the only way that you'll be free
TV's a distraction
We can all do without
Anything that the TV says
Ain't got no real clout
Here's one of my proverbs
If in doubt then just say nowt
It's better to have silent nothings
Than say nothing when you shout.

Andy Senior - HMP Gartree

Prison ... Rehabilitation?

All hope disappeared when I walked down those steps
With life slowly seeping out of me
Just a shadowless ghost
A faceless picture
Led to a place
Where my footsteps no longer leave prints in the snow
Where water never splashes
No matter how hard I fall
Eyes just see through me

A big black hole
Evicted from normality
Starving for affection
Pushed further from reality
Where eyes show no love
And love is just a word
My forgotten existence
Just a fictional character
Lost in a story

Memories of the past only a dream
A fairytale never to be seen
A whole life judged on mistakes
Being suffocated by loneliness
With no air left to breathe
My vision blurred by darkness
Shrinking from confinement
Weighed down by loss

Meaningless time where clocks have no numbers
Voices without ears to listen
A place where rainfall never touches your skin
A colourless sky
Where no birds sing
A place where the grass isn't green
And the sun never shines
Where most are numbed with guilt
Surrounded by stone walls
Echoing its own sadness

Rehabilitation?

Shane - HMP Downview

This is a poem of how prison has made me feel. It is about what prison has taken from me as a person and that I no longer feel there is a place for me, inside or outside here.

Frail and False!

Walking into a rebirth
All was new and colourful
Faster and enjoyable
And the people full of smiles
It was all so frail and false

Encounters were adventure
Each work a gentle pluck
On the nerves of newness
That encouraged each day
It was all so frail and false

Prison is physical and mental
No one expects what they do not know
To carry prison forever on their back
Never finding ground to stand on
It was all so frail and false

Never to repent but always to regret
When a door closed out the whole world
With a slam that breaks the heart
Like the final goodbye to a love
It was all so frail and false

'Sorry' is a womb – echoes that nurture
'think of me long enough to make a memory'

T Shepherd - HMP Barlinnie

A Painful Visit

She's not the mother I used to know
The mother of my childhood
But a hunched and hospitalised old woman
More like my grandmother than my mother!

I recall how, when I was young
She was always bright and busy
(And never ill) – humming away to herself
While she tackled her tasks

Now, as she shuffles slowly into the visits hall
And cranes up at me with eyes
Full of timorous love and unspoken sadness
It's as much as I can do not to break down

Robert Shreeve - HMP Swaleside

The Lost Years

Deep in a dream,
I stood accused of wasting time
and was swept away downstream,
far from familiar sights
and intended destinations,
to the bottom of all nights;
where, floundering among the dross,
the damaged and dead things,
I faced the true enormity of my loss.

Robert Shreeve - HMP Swaleside

What she says (and what she does)

She says she loves,
She says she'll wait,
That her position
Won't ever deviate.
But, she says she likes
Scarves and shampoos,
Then buys another
Pair of shoes!
She says she prefers
Her meals plain,
Then goes on
A rich binge again.
She says she considers
Sport the dregs,
Then runs after
Rugby players' legs.
She says she's happy;
That her heart sings,
But then ... she says
A lot of things.

Robert Shreeve -
HMP Swaleside

Hardman

I don't care,
But I do.
I don't share,
This is for you.

I can't cry,
See my dry tears.
I don't get lonely,
'Hey!' I'm here.

I don't shine,
Can you see?
I don't do deep,
Are you at sea?

I don't do loving,
Let us flame bright.
I don't miss you,
You're coming? Right?

Jason Smith -
HMP Stafford

In my cell

Sun shines past the bars,
bells ring from not far,
marathon runners inspire this day
whilst time is ticking, ticking away.

Traffic hums its background murmur,
carries thoughts to the ones we love,
propels deep regrets
and shouts, I am waiting, I am here.

Siren sounds and hearts skip beats,
reminiscing laboured breath and pounding feet
burning to out-run all that's passed
burning remembrance of the past.

Coldness enfolds and darkness shrouds
like a vacuum light diminishes here
long shadows herald the night
long shadows herald this longest night.

Jason Smith - HMP Stafford

Voyage

Drenching rains, Indian summers
Cast adrift far from land-lubbers
Siren sounds singing to tease
Hurricane's blending into breeze

Shining bright in starlit throne
North star guiding man alone
The great majesty of a moon
Inspiring light from inner gloom

Beacon bathing stormy green
Glancing rocks can now be seen
Lapping waves a peaceful time
Land ahoy, I'll see home soon.

Jason Smith - HMP Stafford

I'm So Glad I Found You

I had waited so very long
To meet someone like you.
Having met with only falsehoods
Whilst searching for the true.

I was just like a traveller
Who had somehow lost their way
And who had suddenly awoken
To a beautiful new day.

My heart is filled with joy for
In everything we share
I find a meaning in each day
That is quite beyond compare.

I know that the love we have
Is all true love can be
For in you I've found my
'Soulmate' the other half of me.

Katie Smith - HMP Newhall

Sent in on Katie's behalf by Simon at HMP Hull

Ignorant Bliss

I'm living in dreams
And always in trouble
Can't deal with my life
So I bring in a double

A life in two halves
Welded together
Two different people
Together forever

Never been me
Always something contrived
Don't even know
If the real me's alive

A necessary evil
Used for only defence
Became my undoing
It doesn't make sense

Too late to turn back
Can't tell them apart
They're both in my head
And both in my heart

Two jigsaws one box
No reason no rhyme
Must I sort out the pictures one at a time

If I put them together
Would I like what I see
Would I make it alone
With only one me

Do I really want answers
Or ignorant bliss
Would I choose the right one
Or the one that I miss

Gerald Smith - HMP Birmingham

Lonely Noel

Christmas getting close
Kids are all excited
Counting down the hours
Myself I'm not invited

I'm sitting in a prison
Feeling sorry for myself
No tree no decorations
And no stocking on the shelf

No searching in the shops
For the perfect little gift
The one you know will do the trick
Give the saddest heart a lift

No mistletoe no kisses
Just a room without a view
No happy children's faces
As their presents they undo

No family at the table
With crackers there to pull
Paper hats and toys
Eating turkey till they're full

Still the table's set at our house
As the kids they sit and wait
For Granddad and his carving knife
I'm afraid I will be late

In fact I won't be coming
Though I send my heartfelt wishes
For a very Merry Christmas
To you all with love and kisses

Gerald Smith -
HMP Birmingham

The Pigeon

A pigeon sat on razor wire
The picture says it all
Looking in the dungeons
Behind the prison wall

In each window there's a convict
But the pigeon doesn't mind
To him they're just a shelter
And convicts can be kind

He sits there like a symbol
Of everything that's free
Put some breadcrumbs on the sill
And freedom comes to me

In a gentle voice I talk to him
While he sits and cocks his head
He shares with me his freedom
I share with him my bread

Then the moment's gone, he lifts
   his wings
And flies back to the wall
A pigeon sat on razor wire
The picture says it all

Gerald Smith -
HMP Birmingham

The Visit

The visit's a pleasure
That comes once a week
A time for comfort
And solace to seek

A chance to hold you
And look in your eyes
See my reflection
Without the disguise

They're not always perfect
But the feelings are true
Conflict or peace
It's still me and you

Cards on the table
Hearts on our sleeve
For better or worse
In this we believe

Sometimes we sit
Hiding heartache with smiles
Walking on eggshells
After travelling miles

The most genuine motives
Still causing pain
A smile without honesty
Is a cloud without rain

These well meaning visits
Do no good at all
We part with a kiss
Then bounce off the walls

Head full of thoughts
All left unsaid
Emotions and feelings
Took over instead

In a beautiful sky
Clouds float through the air
But take away rain
And they wouldn't be there

Well the visit is over
The end of the rhyme
See ya next week
Same prison same time

Gerald Smith - HMP Birmingham

To Answer the Question

I've been on this earth
For what seems like an age
In the grand scheme of life
I might fill a page

I've danced with the devil
Good sense I have spurned
And you can't play with fire
Without getting burned

People have asked me
What would I change
If I lived my life over
What would I rearrange

When they ask me this question
I ask one in return
If you can't make mistakes
Then how do you learn

If the answers are there
On the back of the page
Then why should you struggle
To reach an old age

Pass down your experience
From father to son
To help them in life
When your life is done

They'd simply be born
With the knowledge in mind
No looking forward
When the view's all behind

But to answer the question
I really don't know
I throw seeds to the wind
And reap what I sow

Gerald Smith - HMP Birmingham

Old Lags

Hello there John, how are you son?
Who me? I'm doing fine!
When did we last meet?
In Parkhurst ... '69!
I saw old Jim in Pentonville he's having it with mugs
They nicked him down the Old Kent Road
With a joey full of drugs;
Who? Tony? Ain't you heard? He's dead,
Shot down at Shooters Hill,
It's getting very hard to tell the villains from the Bill.
You hear about Little Freddie?
He's buggered off to Spain,
Apparently he had quite a touch,
Now he's on the gravy train!
Old Charlie copped a seven
They caught him dealing 'blow',
Fifty-seven kilos in a lock-up near Heathrow;
Who me? Yeah, I been stitched right up,
It's funny you should ask,
I'm here for what I didn't do,
I didn't wear a mask!
All right my son be lucky, I'll see you on the yard,
We'll chat about the good old days
And how the game is getting hard;
Don't mention all the wasted years,
The empty days and nights,
The riots and the suicides,
The murders and the fights;
No, we'll just talk of robbing banks
Flying lead and grassing slags,
As we shuffle round the exercise yard,
Just a couple of tired old lags.

Noel 'Razor' Smith - HMP Blantyre House

The Hanging Basket
Seeds of Hope

Vibrant life exploding into colour;
Lavender bordering on white; nearly summer.
Scarlet red; cornflower blues
Primrose yellow – all kinds of hues.
The smell of life; the smell of peace.
The smell of hope; that comes with release.
Warmth of colour, coolness of touch
Such amazing beauty is almost too much.
Though the soil in the basket gets into my nails
The hope of the future will always prevail.

Sol, Wayne, Mark, Jahbi, Sed -
HMP Grendon

A dark place

There's a place in me that's dark and bad,
Memories that make me mad,
Images and thoughts that make me wrong,
Anger aggression once weak now strong,
No outlet for my rage inside,
The emotions I carry I try to hide,
No bags to punch or pads to kick,
The things I feel would make you sick,
Revenge I plot as I lay in my bed,
How did this poison get in my head,
Outside I was content and calm,
Wouldn't wish no-one no harm,
But now a fire burns within,
That makes me want to hurt and sin.

Ross Spencer - HMP Kennet

Skag Rat

Hey there Ratty boy
Hanging on the bars
Calling up the other spur
Asking where they are
Swearing lots of promises
On your baby's life
Don't worry 'bout the consequences
Just deal with the strife.
Get that boot inside you,
Forget the MDTs
You're on a recall anyway
You won't get extra days.
You know you won't do PASRO
And forget the SDPs
In the college of the criminal
You've got all that you need.
You've got your lies, your cheating
You even believe your blags
'Just so long as I'm alright Jack
Fuck the other lags!'
'There's a ton on my canteen sheet''
'My wife's coming with an eighth'
'Just give me what I want right now
We''ll settle up another day'
So if you get a kicking, well
It's cheaper than a score
And a broken nose will always fix
And won't hurt after a roar!

Tony Standen - HMP Elmley

Why

Why am I here looking into space?
What did I really do wrong?
Why would I kill the man I loved?
When he really did me harm
Why did I let him charm me,
With his laughter and his smiles?
Why did I trust and care for him?
Would this feeling go on?
All I know that now he's gone
I'm hurt and totally worn
Too ashamed to show my face
To people that I knew
Knowing what they might think of me
Please don't let this come true
Will these feelings still be with me
When I finally get out of here
With memories of the past?
Will he ever fade from my dreams
And leave me alone at last?

Anne Stanmore - HMP Holloway

You

In the morning I don't eat
Because I think of you

In the afternoon I don't eat
Because I think of you

In the evening I don't eat
Because I think of you

And at night I don't sleep
Because I'm hungry!

Paul Stellato -
HMP Woodhill

Heartache

My home is one of heartache
A place of steel and stone
Just one cell that place is hell
And there I sit alone
For one mistake I pay with time
Where no man wants to be
I smell the fear and shed a tear
Which no one else must see
My body cramps from cold and damp
That chills me to the bone
Although I'm forced to stay here
It will never be my home
I hear the ring the metal swing
Of keys in metal locks
The scrape of feet upon concrete
As screws patrol the blocks
At times I rage and pace that cage
Where no place holds more danger
But although it is a lonely place
I must remain a stranger
I pass my days behind the wall
I'm longing to be free
And when I am my life will start
My place is out there somewhere to be free

Stephen - HMP Ashwell

Cold Steel

Ruined, broken, beyond repair?
Crooked headway to despair
Deconstructed shivered life
Flesh seeps red, cold steel knife,
One or two? No, six deep holes
Glistening anatomy, it's exposed
Deepest, darkest fear the fear,
Cold steel blade held so dear.
Locked away inside a mind
Liquid damaged, cops did find
Flashing blue, riot smash
Storm troop boot, rushing gash
Freezing icicle raindrop fall
Naked, white suit, prison hall.
Years now gone still so raw
Wounds hurting? Even more
Will you, won't you, do you know?
Cold steel blade, puppet show.

'Sticks' - HMP Birmingham

Dreams

Although my cell is dark and small
I dream of dreams beyond the wall
Because my sentence may be long
Don't block the blackbird's song
The judge decreed I may have sinned
But let him try and stop the wind
The moon's still there, so is the sun
And still they will when sentence done
So why not dream of what it's like
To fly a kite or ride a bike
Or win a goldfish at the fair
When sentence done it's still all there

Syd - HMP Wellingborough

Only you

Feeling low, feeling high
Someone scream, someone cry.
No more friends, new regime
Only you and black dark dream.

Stop and stare, court goes shy
No more questions ...when and why.
Sun goes down, kiss goodbye
You know better, not to lie.

Monday, Friday, Saturday
Every minute same old day.
Hell on earth, no more light
Only you and long grey night.

Why you here, what's your crime
No more women, drinks with lime
It is nightmare for your meal
Only you and ... devil's will.

Peter Szczepanski - HMP Belmarsh

Life Through My Eyes

Life through my eyes would scare any man to death
Poverty, murder, violence and never a moment to rest
Fun and games are few but treasured like gold to me
Coz I realise that I must return to my spot in poverty
But hark my words when I say my heart will not exist
Unless my destiny comes through and puts an end to all of this

Ste Tallby - HMP Risley

Inmates come and go

Inmates come and go here day and night
Some are just friends but others form bonds with us.
We share our bitterness, cases and legal jargons
Passing hands of help in emotional crisis
They support you, when found guilty
Desolate partners may desert you
But inmates never leave you
Play games of chess or dominos together
Ping pong or pool tables may be battlefields
But our spirits are high and playful.
Some win with animosity and others with mutual respect
When we have got closer
The call to go home comes sooner
Slipped out to another place suddenly
Our eyes start shedding tears
That can be a mixture of both joy and sorrow.

Neil Tangotra - HMP Pentonville

Love has a price!

You are far but still near to me.
You are arrogant but still dear to me.
You are away like a high mountain
But flows like a serene river near me.
My patience and endurance has run out
Like a midnight piano, you play with me
Floating above the water by a thin thread
My emotions, out of tune, sink and scatter
Outwardly, my conviviality may fool others
As I contrive to uplift my ruinous soul
I would live as long as I feel your love,
But perish the day you stop loving me.
What benefits my love has for you?
No interest, no profit, but only loss
Go away, if you want or if you can,
No chains, no hurts, no ill feelings
As the high rewards come with patience
Which may be round the corner?

Neil Tangotra - HMP Pentonville

A Druggie's Life

Late at night in your cell
Do you ever think back to times that were well?
When ya start off young smoking draw,
Totally untouchable to the law,
Skippin school 'n sniffin' glue
Wiv not a care in what you do.
Then as a dare or maybe a bet
Ya tell ya pal 'pass me that phet',
Off ya go ravin' – ya life re-arranging
The buzz soon goes it's not the same
Need more narcotics for the brain.
'Try this bro' it's an ecstasy pill
Soon be back with a different frill,
Oh my God! What a feeling
Bouncing hard on the fuckin' ceiling,
This life aint no joke
What's that bro, is it coke?
That's it then, you're at the top
You don't want this feeling to ever stop,
Then it happens, ya feel like a clown
Ya turn all paranoid on ya come down,
Head's all tangled, what shall I do?
I know, I'll see Bazza, he used to do this too!
So off I go to knock on his door
With really no clue of what is in store,
'Ere ya go kidda, grab this foil'
It wont be long before ya feeling royal.
It's so true in what he said
This is great, I'm off me fuckin' head.
Then as the days start to trickle by
You notice the sneezes 'n the tears in ya eyes,
The crime gets bigger, got more daring
Shoplifting's gone you've got into burgling,
Then you do the worst you've committed the sin
You've only got ya self hooked on the pin;
That's it then, totally off the wall,
No job too big, no job too small.
The dealer chucks you a bit of crack
That's it then, no looking back;
Burglaries here, robberies there
DNA splashed around everywhere,

Then you do the dealer with a bat
'Fuck him anyway, he's only a twat'
But the snake tells the cops
That's it now ya well on top
Totally under this drug-ridden spell
Two weeks after, ya up in the cell,
So that's got ya thinking of where ya been
And what you've done
But looking back – what great fun!

Neil Taylor - HMP Moorland

Old Soldiers Never Cry

Homeless, jobless, on the street
One of 'those' that you don't meet
It's hard when you are out of luck
Run out of cash and you are stuck

No place to sleep, completely broke
No cash for food and not one smoke
'It's his own fault' I hear you say
To me it doesn't seem that way

When I left school they thought me barmy
Five A levels gained I joined the army
They taught me to fight and how to kill
Said 'it's just survival skill'

I quickly learned all that they taught
Sent abroad where I lived and fought
I did well, good at my job
They'd changed me from a teenage yob

I came back for a ten day leave
Some R & R and some time to grieve
For good mates I'd left behind
Dead, disabled and some were blind

I went out for a quiet drink
On my own so that I could think
I had two drinks stood at the bar
My thoughts had wandered off afar

Behind I heard sounds of a fight
Started to turn round to my right
A hard blow landed on my face
My heart and blood began to race

Instinct kicked in, I threw a chop
Shit hit the fan, it was a cop
I didn't think, just trained reaction
It put him down and then in traction

My brief knew this and told the judge
But he'd scented blood and wouldn't budge

➤

He wouldn't even give me bail
I spent ten years in a poxy jail

In uniform it's not a crime
In civvie street they give you time
They try to get into your head
But I switched off, emotion dead

Career busted, family gone
She just sent me a 'Dear John'
Done my time and now I'm out
So you tell me what it's all about

I served my country, paid my dues
But still condemned to bloody lose
I think my life's come to an end
What kind of message does this send?

Seems to me that what it means
If you are fit and full of beans
Don't learn skills that rule your head
Or very soon someone is dead

Mike Taylor - HMP Albany

Stop The Clock

The beauty of imagination
Close your eyes make it happen
In my dream the setting is perfect
No quarrels to settle, no reason to fight
The real deal, the right deal
No tears to dry, no broken heart to heal
Her smile is a window that lets me see
Her heart is at home for me
Eyes like sparkling diamonds set in
Polished white stone
She holds herself like a swan gracing water
A match like the prodigal son dating a king's daughter
Go your own way my lover, lets not
Shatter this dream
And when you close your eyes, remember we're a team.

Graeme Taylor - HMP Nottingham

Different kinds of everyone

Transfixed? Beyond redemption?
Was there nothing left to say?
In vivid times, the sun won't shine
As the days lay mesmerised.
We were different kinds of everyone
In a place that some belonged
With multi-cells of evidence
And keys that had no notes.
We each reflect like beacons
Our stories as they unfold
For some are said in ego
And some could not be told.
Those steps on forever landings
That lead some round the bend
And others conned by demons
For them there was no end.
Of time and forced to look inside
All memories of past to view
In lives, no words of wisdom
Just chips and veg to stew.
Were we all but at the brink?
On a ship that sailed no sea
Full of different kinds of everyone
Just wishing they were free.
As the tick had lost its tock
And the glass misplaced, no hour
The bolts replaced by screws
In ice they took to shower.
From sweat they came in boxes
For pence they worked with no complaint
In church they passed the parcel
And everyone a Saint.
As each was checked by roll
All names arithmetic
And mirrored in the classes
For some were far from thick.
Just wasted with no belonging
Or a fuse that was far from tall
We were different kinds of everyone
Just trying not to fall.

Liam Thomas - HMP Shrewsbury

A Seasonal Sense of Freedom

With misted eyes, I watch the waning sun,
Baptism for my heart in molten gold,
Another slow October's day undone,
In silent stealth, night falls; I feel so cold.

My thoughts turn to this season, all it means,
How time itself feels old, this time of year,
As leaves of red and gold steal summer's greens,
While winter, wreathed in shadow, inches near.

Still autumn breathes awhile of warm romance,
Lost spirits reminisce on what has been,
To bonfires, errant souls are drawn to dance,
For haunted hearts hold sway at Halloween.

Ghost scents and childhood's laughter come to me,
The captive deep within myself breaks free.

Jason Thompson - HMP Maghaberry

Please answer me

I'm lost, I'm scared
I'm so full of pain
I let myself down
Again and again

I'm tired, I'm lonely
I'm full of regret
I'm caught up here
In a fishing net

Can anyone save me?
Can anyone help?
I've got so many problems
But no one to tell

Somebody, anybody
Can anyone hear?
I can't do this alone
It's too much to bear

I'm lost, I'm scared
Did I do this to myself?
Someone please answer me
I need your help

Mum … answer my calls
God … answer my prayers
Friends … answer my questions
I need to know if you're there.

Danyella Thompson -
HMP Send

Hewell Holiday Complex
'you can check out anytime you like,
but you can never leave'

HMP, the place to be, it really is a scream
The rooms are great, the staff polite, everyday's a dream
Wake each day, put on TV, get breakfast served in bed
Shall we have full English or have cheese like on the Med

Up at ten, get washed and dressed, then amble into work
There's quite a mix of guests in here, Chinese, Asian, Turk
Knock off at twelve and wander back, look forward to your meal
After that we sleep or work, depending how we feel

Dinner time's a real treat, the food is a la carte
A cornucopia of delicacies, you don't know where to start
Evening time we smoke cigars, drink brandy, rum or port
Shall we have a rest tonight or join in all the sport

Chew the fat, get massaged or the bubble spa
Or nip down to the local pub in the company car
Night time comes and so to bed, you'll never find a bug
If you believe a word of this, you're just a f***in mug!

Adrian Tinson - HMP Hewell

One More Time

Nothing I must do
Nowhere I should be
No one in my life to answer to, but me
No more candlelight
No more purple skies
No one to be near
As my heart slowly dies
I've memorized your face
I know your touch by heart
Still lasting your embrace
I'd dream of where you are
If I could hold you one more time
Like in the days when you were mine
I'd look at you till I was blind
So you would stay
I'd say a prayer each time you smile
Cradle the moments like a child
I'd stop the world if only I could
Hold you one more time

Felipe Tripicchio - HMP The Mount

Window Warrior

Every night you hear the window warrior
Warbling 'cock a doodle do'
Nose pressed to the window
As if stuck by super glue

He's won more fights than Tyson
In or out the ring
No rap star has more diamonds
Gold or blazing bling.

Fast cars and racy women
He's nicked and had 'em all
I love his bragging stories
Even if they're tall.

The screws have gone on strike
It's bang up for the day
Where are you window warrior?
Please come out to play

Nothing on the telly
Nothing else to do
Thank God for window warrior
Twittering right on cue!

Andy Tuffs - HMP Brixton

Application Procedure

Nine months ago I made an app
for a pencil set, nothing crap.
Still I wait, one app per month
two formal complaints and nothing back

I'm in art ed. you see
and rules are rules
'No art materials to be removed'
So just a pencil set to help me out
when in my pad with no way out
Drawing pads, erasers too
can be had on canteen
But pencils no, they can't be seen!

So I made my app cat order too.
Nothing happens! So made another
and another and yet another.

In the end I'd had enough
the apps weren't getting through
Formal complaint number one came back
'No order seen, make out an app'

Formal complaint number two came back
'No trace of apps. We need to know
what apps you've made before you have a go'.

Nine copies made and sent in
At last the money's gone, it won't be long
Three weeks on but no pencils yet!
Guess what? I have to make an app!

Basic pencil set first requested 07.08.07 from
Argos. Finally received 13.4.08!

Steve Twigg - HMP Hull

Bang Up Blues

'Well I never felt more like singing the blues'
That colour, I'm sure is a plot by the screws,
Used by the head shrinkers to brainwash us lot,
To mess with our Swedes, a devilish plot!

Blue is a cold colour, it makes you think - ICE!
Booze in a blue bottle – Wicked! Cool and nice!
Those songs like Blue Velvet, Blue Moon, Blue Bayou
Imply heartbreak, sadness, feelings we all knew!

Some bird, name of Venus, wore jeans coloured blue,
She sounds like a fit bit, enjoys a good screw!
That cheers up the soul, the sap starts to rise,
But only exists – in minds, not in eyes!!

Yes! Blue is a bummer, I think we agree,
I've glanced round my sad pad, I'll list what I see,
Light blue backed front door, dark blue skirting board,
I'm inside a freezer! Where dead meat is stored!

One colour that stunts our battered taste buds,
They've given us blue plates, bowls, spoons and blue mugs,
They dress us in 'frost kit', blue tee shirts, blue kecks,
They might as well pack ice cubes down our necks!

It's funny but green says 'Peace' 'Rest' calming!
Green trees inspire painters – one once saved a king!
Green grass fires up poets, those planters of words,
It's got good food value – it feeds cattle herds.

Green veg and green salad, the things Mam said 'Eat!'
She knew they were healthy, when served up with meat.
We eat with our eyes, so tell me when you,
Last ate blue pig sausage or Irish blue stew?

I'll wrap up with sport, a team from Eastlands
Man City, those Sky Blues, no 'red' on their hands
I've watched them for years - Mancunians - true,
But sometimes their score cards have made ME feel blue!

Reds are communists, flags, uniforms, blood,
The colour of fire, sun rises, hot mud,
'cos red inspires action, war, battle, movement,
You wont see much red here, it might cause ferment!

P Vernon - HMP Manchester

Sycamore tree

Reason is like a bunch of grapes
Not one reason but many
Retribution is the lace of a shoe
Which does up
But can't undo
All the troubles in the past.
Regret is the hand to help you undo the knot
Reconciliation is tying up all the loose ends
Remorse is not regret but should mean compassion
Repentance is a pen to write down all ones wrongs
Restoration is a page in a book that can't be closed
Restitution means giving back all the things I have taken
Reparation is like a tree
That re-grows when it is broken
Responsibilities are the roots that keep you strong
Salvation is a feather that gives the angels flight
Forgiveness is a door to peace and happiness
Change is the key, a key to a whole new world.

Corinne Vincent - HMP Holloway

Abandonment

I'm coming home, it's been too long
I've missed you so much
Your kind smile, beautiful hair and loving touch
While together we become as one
A knot pulled tight, forcibly undone
My heart can sense it, the time is near
The sky is a perfect blue, the air is clear
The sun shines, the birds are in full song
I'm coming home, it's been too long

Matthew Walsh - HMP Camp Hill

Cell with a view

Stood here at the top of this hill,
Peering through bars and rings of steel,
Looking out over tall swaying trees,
Stood naked in grief with the loss of their leaves,
My thoughts drift off on the cool winter breeze,
A million miles from crooks and thieves

Circling above gathering to roost,
Hundreds and hundreds of jackdaws and rooks
Gathered together they fly with such grace
The extent of their freedom,
Rubbed in my face.

Matthew Walsh - HMP Camp Hill

Over

I phone my wife, engaged!
I hang up 'SLAM' enraged!
Four times today
It's been this way
Frustration doubles, caged

A VO sent; ignored
She writes to me 'I'm bored'
And now she's gone
And left this con,
The man she once adored

She's working now, employed
The West End shops enjoyed
She don't need me
She's been set free
Relationship destroyed

George Watts -
HMP Pentonville

Doing time

Doing time is a funny place, a different storm
Behind every face. The strong, the weak, the timid,
The shamed.

In each prison they're all the same. The predators
Prowl, the victims weak, there's many who will
Find no sleep.

Each day a sentence of its own, they've got no one
Out there, nobody to phone. Let's face the truth
They're on their own.

Alone at night, no use for the bed, just the
Fears and worries, going round in their head.

Each morning brings a brand new day, don't know
Who to talk to, wouldn't know what to say.

The judge passed the sentence, he thought it
Was swell, not realising how many he sends
Into hell.

Some never make it, it's where lives can end,
But when you hear the statistics, it's how many
They mend.

Yes, doing time is a funny old place, with a
Different story behind every face.

Haige White - HMP Chelmsford

Television Hell

I've never watched so much TV,
Since that judge imprisoned me.
They put me in a prison cell,
With a man from TV hell.
A true original soap queen,
With eyes alive like a TV screen.
9.15 in the morning on BBC 1
He starts with Don't get Done, get Dom
Next is Homes under the Hammer
This guy's a human TV planner,
He doesn't need a TV guide,
As he waits for To Buy or not to Buy,
Then as that programme's credits flash
He says 'yeah, let's watch Trash for Cash.
By now its true, I've got the hump,
Cos this dude's watching Bargain Hunt
And on each break, just for a while
He'll flick over to catch bits of Jeremy Kyle.
Now I'm so bored I take a snooze
And in my dreams I see the news.
As he sat down to his mid-day meal
Mesmerised by Dickinson's Deal,
Then just before its time for labour
He's settled in for watching Neighbours.
It's on twice, like Home and Away,
But he wants to watch Golden Balls later today.
So I ask 'hey can I watch Countdown?
He says 'no, sorry cos I watch Lazytown.
I said 'what's that?', He says 'a cartoon,
I watch C-Beebies all afternoon'.
So by the time it gets to five o'clock,
I'm ready to knock off his block.
I read for a bit cos there's no interaction,
But Jasper Carrot's voice is causing a distraction.
With the Simpsons at six, cell mates gone for a shower,
But he's back for Hollyoaks, in half an hour.
Not long after that I admitted defeat,
Cos Emmerdale was followed by Coronation Street.
I can handle an episode of The Bill,
But there was a question bugging me still,
I may as well ask, and seize the day,
'What's your favourite film mate?'
He said 'Groundhog Day!'

Luke Whiteman - HMP Leicester

Through new eyes!

I used to be completely cruel, a heartless arse,
Using people and girls and then tossing them aside.
I used to feel an angry, bitter, hunger,
Not knowing why, I'd just tell lies.
I used to think the goal of life was pleasure,
My own of course
No matter, whatever.
I hunted for my lonely ecstasy and
Even when I wanted to be in company
The only one I cared about was me!
A woman's feelings had to be her own problem,
Her mistake.
We make our own world and mine was full
Of other fools to be used,
Or girls to be screwed.
I'd take my pleasure they'd take theirs
But never unified,
Just something to pass the time.
And then I fell in love with you,
And somehow your happiness meant more to me than mine,
All this time I'd been drinking wine,
Acting like a swine
Now I'm with you and looking through different eyes,
And I can't help but realise,
I wanna keep you so there'll be no more lies.

Gary Wilkinson- HMP Elmley

Sick Building Syndrome

This building is sick.
Choked by smoke,
Bruised and beaten,
Hated to its core.

Bitten by saws,
Dug at by picks,
Smeared with shite,
And at night ...

Tossing with fever
Dreams of death, of capture,
Of the rapture of pain
Of blame
Of Always The Same.

Dreaming of sex,
Slick with sterile wet patches
And snatches
Of worlds all but lost
Drowned
Worlds bound.

This building is ill.
Its cells are diseased,
Throwing up from emotion sickness,
Drugged with misery.

Scabbed over.
It's terminal. It's had its chips.
(Every weekday teatime meal – without fail).
This building looks decidedly pale.

A landfill that reeks of derelict men
Of piss and smoke
Of cabbages and blokes
This building's got a carcinoma –
A malignant growth,
Murderous sloth.

Don't breathe its air.

The future's being shaped in there.

Matthew Williams - HMP Stocken

Evening calling

There's a dull glimmer tonight
In the misty dark
Draped in twilight's shadow
Memory haunts and leaves its mark

Faces and times in a vision
Like a thousand yard stare
The ghostly congregation
Leads to who knows where

As life becomes dust
For the moonlight to drink
The last grains of night
On a silver ribbon, sink

Like a yacht on another journey
Ocean salt tears drifting
Empty quayside of feelings
No shore, nor harbour uplifting

I have seen life madly beautiful
Now I have nothing anymore
All that's left is memories
Of all that went before

Solitude of evening
Retains heartaches you cannot outrun
Is there anything left to believe in
With so much damage done

Kevin Willis - HMP Gloucester

Sorry

Went to the pub for a drink or two,
This guy spilt his drink on my shoe,
While thinking to myself what shall I do,
This guy got an attitude,
So I see red,
Give him a dig in the head.
He's lucky he's not dead,
He's resting in a bed,
Now I am filled with dread.

He took me to court,
Who would of thought,
That this kind of guy was pleasant and shy,
The judge asked me
Why couldn't I say nothing just cry,
Watching my girl say bye bye!

Now I'm sitting in my cell,
It's a place from hell,
With nothing to do,
Just thinking of you and my kids
I've got two,
Shit, I should of knew
But now what can I do
Part from say sorry to you.

Clayton Wilson –
HMP Wellingborough

What's Missing?

I miss the smell of petrol fumes;
Hearing mobile phones ringing.
I miss pub karaoke,
With all the tone deaf singing.

I miss the sound of sea and shingle,
As I take my seafront stroll.
I miss pensioners in white,
Playing crown green bowls.

I miss the children's laughter
As they run and lark about;
I miss the sound of mums and dads
As they get annoyed and shout.

I miss those long promenades,
That encourage me to run.
I miss driving up to Beachy Head
To watch the setting sun.

I miss gym in the morning
And all that early training;
I miss running to the car,
Even when it's raining.

I miss satellite television,
Sky Sports and Setanta.
I miss watching football with mates
With all that friendly banter.

I miss the crowded motorways
Whilst driving to see my folks.
I even miss the road rage
From young, impatient blokes.

I miss the sound of cutlery
As it clunks against the plate.
I miss homemade spaghetti Bolognese
That my friends highly rate.

➤

I miss the taste of ice cream,
Of peaches and white wine.
I miss the friendly restaurants,
Where the food is just divine.

I miss summer cricket,
Or Sundays in the park;
Lying on lush green grass,
Not leaving till it's dark.

I miss so much of everything
In Prison.

Geoff Wilson - HMP Albany

From young, impatient blokes

I miss the sound of cutlery
As it clunks against the plate.
I miss homemade spaghetti Bolognese
That my friends highly rate.

I miss the taste of ice cream,
Of peaches and white wine.
I miss the friendly restaurants,
Where the food is just divine.

I miss summer cricket,
Or Sundays in the park;
Lying on lush green grass,
Not leaving till it's dark.

I miss so much of everything
In Prison.

Geoff Wilson - HMP Albany

Rat Race

You took over my life and made me your slave,
I was out every night, looking for a raze,
Breaking the law, so that I could score,
To make me feel good once more,
The mental side was bad enough,
But the physical side was pretty rough,
And if I woke without any gear,
I'd pick up the phone and put it to my ear,
I'd start the day with bag number one,
'Where is the next one coming from?'
The months flew by as I lost track of time,
And I ended up addicted to crime,
I worked for you like you were my boss,
But without any wages or any days off,
When I got in I could finally sit,
Mission complete, my reward was a hit,
I'd be ok for a couple of hours,
But after that, things could turn sour,
My nose will be dripping, my legs like jelly,
I'll be feeling the pain from the cramps in my belly,
And that's just the start of what you would do,
The first withdrawals felt like the flu,
You had me locked up by a fiery chain
And burnt me bad if I didn't play your game
You put me in pain,
Drove me insane,
And I've only got myself to blame,
I damaged myself and others around,
And all I needed was another ten pounds,
My family and friends had just given up,
On feeding my habit or watching me cluck,
I tried to get help but my local town,
Has too many people addicted to brown,
They told me six months of waiting in line,
And sent me back to drugs and crime,
Now I'm back behind bricks and steel,
And all because of a ten pound deal,
They put me on meth straight away,
I started a script the following day,
You've gone for good and the meds have stopped
I might be locked up but you can't stop the clock
The chains are gone
There's no more burning
At last is seems the tables are turning

Ben Woodfield – HMP Prescoed

TWOC

I'm a twocer, the best there is
Night or day I'll take the piss
No doubt about it's all a laugh
Before I go I'll smoke some grass
When night falls I'm ready to start
I creep about in the dark
Over the BMX track and through the park
And around the corner is where I lark
I see an Audi which looks alright
Obviously I'm back later that night
In the window and out with the keys
In the car and off down the streets
Through first and second I'm hitting fifty
I like the car it's pretty nifty
On the A46 I'm hitting 135
I've never felt so alive
Got into Lincoln and a fed spins around
Got chased into town
Ditched the car and got on my toes
Got gripped up and wished I'd dusted those
Now in jail and looking at a stretch
But not to worry I'll ride whatever I get

Sean Woolley - HMP Stocken

Prison Boy

There was a simple prison boy
Who lived a life of lonesome joy
He messed about and liked a lark
But mad thoughts would come in the dark
So in his cell cold and glum
With lack of sex, drugs and rum
He put a razor to his vein
And no one spoke of him again.

David Wright - HMP Belmarsh

Our Hero - Olympics

Bow your head for medal deserved –
For years of hard work and devotion,
Flag gets raised – hand on heart –
Overwhelmed with emotion,
Embrace your fellow recipients,
Your superman feelings unfold,
They have Bronze and Silver –
But you've got ultimate Gold.
Chest stuck out and arms raised –
For joyous celebration,
Banners waft and flags glide swiftly
From a hundred different nations.
You step down from your podium,
Shoulders swathed with Union Jack,
Now a lap of honour's required of you,
To let them know you're back.
For in the past you've been an idol –
Until you failed to deliver,
Now you've shown what you can achieve –
Your spirit never withered.
People dismissed you when you failed,
Their feelings quite abrupt,
But now you are their Hero –
Just listen to the stadium erupt.

Michael Wyatt - HMP Long Lartin

Cockroach in my pad

I found a little cockroach in my pad,
And he was dancing, round and round like mad,
I said easy roachy wots the score
He said yes now Youngy I've got some draw
I soon found out he was not joking
So we started some serious smoking!
I didn't go to sleep till just gone eleven
And didn't wake up till way past seven
When I woke up he was still there
Sniffing lines of coke off my chair!
I said hey little cockroach sort us a snorter
He said ok Youngy here's a quarter!
And then he said would I like a rave?
Because he had 2 Es that he'd managed to save!
A couple more lines to blow your mind,
The finest bit of white you will ever find,
So if you see him don't be afraid,
Just ask for a snorter till you get paid!

Anthony Young - HMYOI Deerbolt